The fall of VENICE

Maurice Rowdon

The fall of VENICE

WEIDENFELD AND NICOLSON

5 Winsley Street London W1

SBN 297 00013 6

Printed in Great Britain
by Willmer Brothers Limited, Birkenhead

CONTENTS

....

ILLUSTRATIONS

....

from the island of San Giorgio, from a painting by Canaletto (National Gallery).

Chapter 1

The Thousand-year Fight for Survival

Venice always had the possibilities of magic (both black and white). Her first settlers in the fifth century were refugees from the Italian mainland, when barbarians were pouring south. They chose a strange element – water – as their living place. Attila the Hun is supposed to have said that no grass would ever grow where his horse had passed, and perhaps the Venetians went where no grass grew with this in mind. It was a magical thing to want to plant a city in an immense shallow pool of water, on sand formed by endless river-deposits. It was certainly a magical thing to achieve. Sixty churches fell down before they got it right.

The choice was clever. The sandy shelf of what we now call the Lido barred heavy seas from the pool or *laguna*. Yet in that lagoon there were certain deep channels navigable by boats. If you got there first you naturally found out where these were, and memorised them. Invaders, not knowing them, floundered in the sand. And if they did find a deep entrance to the heart of the lagoon where your settlement lay, you simply blocked it. There lay the key to Venice's survival behind natural barriers for well over a thousand years. Slowly a city came into being between the Alps and the sea, secluded, separate, only half in the world.

Her desire to cut herself off from the mainland became her most mysterious asset: Greek, Arab, Jewish, Turkish and Armenian elements combined not only in the passing population of the Rialto but in her buildings, her ogee windows, in her soft and intimate dialect like the sea itself, that could be treacherous as well, in her prowess that seemed to draw from the Aegean and ancient Greece, in her grim, commercial calculation that drew from the Levant, in her occasional unsparing cruelty that had learned a lesson from Islam.

The remarkable thing was that she started as a refugee and ended with an empire of two million subjects. She turned her peculiar position mid-way between land and sea to use. She built a navy, and by the tenth century was the chief trading link between Europe and the Levant. She was rich and independent. The wealth gave her a taste for empire – that is for permanent trading posts along the Dalmatian coast and south in the Aegean, manned by her own people. Her position as a kind of sea-creature made her the most feared naval power in the early Middle Ages.

Venice was first and last a sea power. In the same century she began to turn her attention to the ports on either side of the Adriatic which were showing, with the gradual dissolution of the Byzantine empire, more and more independence; she looked on their spirit of independence jealously at first, but then with a typical stroke made it the basis of her empire. What authority she had on the Italian mainland was based on her success at sea, on an able fleet and a maritime port linking continental Europe with the eastern empire.

But this life between sea and mainland was a shaky one, and it fell to doge Orseolo's son to do something about it when he became doge in 991: he made a treaty with the Holy Roman Empire and Byzantium in return for the payment of tributes to both. Venice's position as an independent maritime state was recognised. He was the first doge too to use the kind of cunning diplomacy for which Venice was later feared and hated. The Dalmatian ports needed help against pirates, and he gave it to them, and neatly scooped them into his empire at the same time. He became Duke of Dalmatia; Capo d'Istria, Isola, Emone, Rovigno, Humago, Pirano and Zara, Lesina and Ragusa all swore allegiance to this mysterious new sea-power.

But it was the first Crusade at the end of the eleventh century that turned Venice from a makeshift settlement into a centre of luxury where princes and even poets (as long as they were socially recognised) could enjoy themselves as nowhere else in the Christian world. The knights of the Crusade needed Venetian ships to get them to the Holy Places; and the Venetians needed the spoil. That was the wily bargain behind the Crusades. Yet behind the Venetian participation there was more than either Christian zeal or brutal greed. In 1098 when Vitale Michiele was doge, about two hundred ships sailed from the Adriatic, half of them supplied by Dalmatian ports. A carefully considered policy steered a course (though not a very safe one) between the Byzantine emperor, suspicious of so much activity close to his own borders, and the pope, who was wondering why the knights failed to reach their destination. What in fact the knights were doing – rather to even their own surprise – was fighting for the Venetian empire on their way down.

Against the anger of Byzantium and Rome the doge had to offset not only the terrific advantage to Venice of markets all over the eastern Mediterranean but the thought that somebody else might get there first. One of the first things Venice did in this first Crusade was to get herself into a quarrel with her Pisan allies, which resulted in the capture of twenty Pisan galleys and five thousand men. By 1122, under the doge Domenico Michiele, a quarter of Acre had been handed over to her, and a whole street in every city of the kingdom of Jerusalem, with a bakery, bath, a market and a church ; above all, Venetian residents in those places paid no taxes, and their imports passed without duty.

Then, under the same doge, began the slow reduction of another ally, the Greek empire. Rhodes was sacked and pillaged. Doge Michiele attacked the whole of the Archipelago. The best looking youths of both sexes were sold as slaves. The plunder was described as the most fabulous since creation. Under the doge Enrico Dandolo, in the Fourth Crusade, Constantinople was attacked for the first time. The Venetian fleet left Venice on 9 October 1202. Within two years Constantinople had become a sort of spoils market with Venice as the bank. Palaces and churches were stripped to the brick ; solid gold crowns, vessels studded with gems, rings and brooches, sapphires, emeralds, topazes, carpets and tapestries, furs and silks all went into the bag. The four bronze horses that stand above the portals of St Mark's were taken from the Hippodrome. These 'Christians' tore down the Veil of the Sanctuary in Sta Sophia, and smashed up the Altar of the Virgin. It was so busy a market that Venetian merchants had to organise it : they acted as brokers and gave money for spoils, taking a percentage themselves (a measure which they invented, by the way). The pope warned but did not excommunicate, especially as there was a hope that he might get Byzantium, if Venice ruined it efficiently enough.

But Venice proved that she was in the war-game for herself alone ; her relations with Rome were never good as a result ; she was twice excommunicated over the centuries, once in 1309 and once in 1606, though the second time did only the pope damage. Being a maritime power, beholden to no one on the mainland, in contact with other civilisations through her trade, in particular with the Greek Orthodox world where papal dignity meant nothing, Venice always had the seeds of a protestant temper. It was no accident that she reached the height of her power at the time of the Reformation. In the sixteenth century there were over fifteen hundred trials by the Holy Office inside the Republic, in the seventeenth century a hundred less and during the last century of the Republic's life only five hundred and sixty-one ; and most of these last cases were quashed through lack of evidence. Heretics were never burned in Venice, as a point of pride, but murdered in the conventional Venetian style – strangled in their cells, beheaded or secretly drowned. Their bodies were sometimes burned afterwards as a concession. The room where the members of the Inquisition sat was kept gloomy and badly furnished: it was a way of saying that the Church came lower than Venice.

From her first century to her last she had one dominating problem – how to survive. Yet though she could never take her independence for granted, though she was on the point of collapse at some time in every century of her history, though enemies were dying to get at her from every side, she had an astonishing reputation for security. What Président de Brosses said about her in the eighteenth century ('the securest town in Italy') had been said in almost as many words quite four hundred years before. At a time when other Italian states were continually in social chaos or being ravaged by foreigners, she presented a picture of serenity and unassailable self-assurance. It was what drew Petrarch to her, the only poet she ever had. In 1362, from his vast palace on the Riva degli Schiavoni he saw the innumerable vessels which go out in the desolate winter, in the most variable and stormy spring, one turning its prow to the east, the other to the west; some carrying our wine to foam in British cups, our fruit to flatter the palates of the Scythians, and, still harder to believe, the wood of our forests to the Aegean and the Achaian islands; some to Syria, to Armenia, to the Arabs and Persians, carrying oil and linen and saffron, and bringing back all their different goods to us.

It was his social standing, more perhaps than anything to do with taste or scholarship, that got him Venice's hospitality. There was always a desire in the Venetian oligarchy to make their city shine in the world, and to hide their policies under the glitter. One summer evening in 1364 Petrarch was sitting at one of his windows with the Archbishop of Patrae when he saw a galley coming into harbour with streamers trailing from the masts, its seamen garlanded. There had been a victory. Crete had been subdued. And a few days later he watched the celebrations at the doge's side, over the portals of the Basilica. A wooden balcony held forty of the noblest women in Venice, flashing with jewels, despite the strict Sumptuary Law passed less than ten years before. The prize for one of the jousts was a crown of solid gold, studded with precious stones.

Yet it was to celebrate an act of cowardice and, more astonishingly, a victory over fellow-Venetians. For a long time the Venetian population of Crete had been complaining of taxation without representation; they had no say even in their own government, let alone Venice's. The Governor's neat answer – 'Are there any sages among you?' (to their request that twenty Sages be elected from among them to the Great Council) – touched off a rebellion, and the Cretan arsenals were sacked. It took a Venetian fleet of thirty-three galleys and six thousand men just three days to establish order; great numbers were hanged. It was all this that made Petrarch say, 'Venice exults not only over the regained sovereignty of Crete but in the thought that right has been vindicated, that is to say, not in Venice's cause alone but that of justice.'

The senators could be quite stupendously cruel when faced with rebellion. Two massive columns plundered from one of the islands in the Archipelago in an early Crusade were placed at the edge of the

Piazzetta, and made a convenient scaffold. For centuries *essere tra Marco e Todero* ('to be between St Mark and St Theodor', the city's patron saints, represented at the top of the columns) meant 'to be in a tight spot'. In the fifteenth century two priests who treated secretly with the ruling prince of Padua while officially at war with him were buried alive face downwards between them. And the Genoese sailor who swore when he landed on the Molo as a prisoner that he would like nothing better than to wash his hands in the blood of a Venetian was not only hanged but had the soles of his feet cut open so that the stones below were stained with his blood for some weeks afterwards.

These things were nothing to the secret executions kept for leaders of rebellions, for foreign princes and citizens too powerful or popular for the safety of the state. The murder of the prince of Padua, Francesco Novello da Carrara at the beginning of the fifteenth century was one of the most fiendishly heartless in Venetian history. He was slowly throttled with the bow-string, and so were his sons. 'A dead man cannot make war', his worst enemy had told the Senate. The fact was that Padua lay too close to Venice to be allowed a ruler of his brilliance and appeal. Yet he was prince of Padua by blood and general recognition. Not only had Venice always recognised him but the doge's council or Signory had given him a personal safe conduct into the city which he need not have used. He made the mistake of trusting the Serenissima. People made that mistake less and less as time went on. They learned that she observed strict loyalty to her own interests but no others.

These were the interests of all Venetians, though a few families did the ruling, and did it absolutely. The unity of Venetian interests explains why the people never rose up against the senators' cruelties. In fact, their own heroes were always being put on trial; leaders only had to become popular for a trial to be more or less automatic. Even Carlo Zeno got no gratitude for saving Venice from certain downfall in 1380, in the War of Chioggia. He had twice been given up for dead in battles. At his death thirty-five wounds were counted on his body. He had bribed his fickle mercenaries with money from his own pocket. But this did not stop the senators accusing him of cowardice because he refused to let his fleet be massacred in the treacherous marshes at the mouth of the Tagliamento. And much the same happened to Zeno's contemporary Admiral Pisani; like Zeno he never breathed a word of complaint, even when the Signory released him from prison only to fight their battles again. In the War of Chioggia, Venice's worst crisis of any time, only one man, Michele Morosini, was thought to have been unpatriotic (he speculated on the price of houses), and even that may have been the gossip of his enemies. At any rate he was made the next doge, perhaps more to keep out heroes like Carlo Zeno than anything.

The dogeship was, in fact, the one public office where the nobles preferred mediocrity. It became the cover behind which others governed, a sort of mythical state-image kept alive by unsparing pageantry, an elected monarchy more and more hemmed in with constitutional checks and balances, the nearest equivalent in history to the modern president.

Venice's tournaments and fireworks and long holidays were less an aspect of her wealth or even, before the sixteenth century, her desire to influence foreigners, than an intelligent political design. Yet because everyone joined in the pleasures and believed in their city, got rich by trade and only incidentally by bloodshed, the result was nothing grimly or brutally Roman: a certain grace of living permeated the city and touched the manners of its nobles, mellowing and softening them with time; their link with the people came to have a sweetly self-assured arrogance of the kind Italians love in their rulers. It made Venice one family, a remarkably spontaneous one, even sometimes a happy one. That was how foreigners saw her in almost every century after the twelfth.

By the time the families at the top had decided to make themselves a compact and exclusive body governing by hereditary right and inscribed in a Golden Book (1319), markets had been won everywhere in the Levant, and the memory of Venice as a half-beleaguered city of fugitives was dead. The so-called Closing of the Council in 1298 shut the doors of the Great Council against the middle class – and locked new members of the nobility in.

Until then it was never really clear to the ordinary Venetian that he actually *lacked* the right to elect members to the Great Council or even become one himself. It always seemed a logical possibility; only it never happened. And it was this surviving empty belief that the Closing of the Council destroyed. In 1325 a special criminal court of ten magistrates, always called the Ten (*I Dieci*), with emergency powers, was instituted. There was no appeal against their decisions. The only constitutional hold on them was the fact that they were elected by the Great Council, annually and then every six months, and for a limited period which started at ten days and then by stages became permanent. Really it created a police state; and some people date Venice's decline from this point. It was started to stamp out the last traces of a conspiracy in 1310. Everyone outside the nobility now knew that their role was to watch and listen. And it says volumes for the genius of the noble class that the ordinary people and the middle class were happy to do this for another half millennium.

One of the reasons why the nobles lasted as long as they did was their instinct for democracy among themselves. Venice must be the only state in history to have made snobbery illegal. You could get six months stifling under the leads of the ducal palace for boasting about your forbears. And if you did it a second time you could be drowned secretly. No more ascetic class existed in Christendom. As spies were planted everywhere, the idlest remark could get you into trouble with the Ten.

It was in the same epoch that the state started showing anxiety that no one noble family should rise above another. The Sumptuary Laws of 1356 came into being with this in mind. They regulated the jewellery, tables and personal appearance of each class of citizen. Cloaks, even those of the richest nobleman, had to be dark and of Paduan cloth: Venetians could be fined for wearing English, Spanish or Dutch materials.

It was now, towards the end of the fourteenth century, that the nobles began to itch for big possessions on the mainland. The police state turned, as police states will, into a war state. Until now Venice's love of the reckless had been indulged far away in the Morea and the Archipelago, but now she used the mercenary captain Carmagnola in an alliance with Florence against Milan. In other words, she deserted the sea. She threw herself into the mercenary war-market of the time, which was very expensive and needed more experience than she had.

The dark Venice that has frightened historians ever since came into being in the fourteenth century: it was government as conceived by the military, a régime supported by spies and secret murders. The three 'inquisitors of state', as they came to be called, grew out of the Ten, as its secret committee. They began life in the fourteenth century as two men, later three, with the job of proving the guilt of accused persons, and of secretly murdering them when necessary. The troubles of the fourteenth century made them a permanent body, but the very different troubles of the sixteenth (chief among them the fear of Spain) gave them absolute power for the first time, and then for a term of a year. They no longer needed to consult the Ten, and their archives were secret. The fear that Spanish dominion in Italy would soon spread to the independent Italian states (Savoy and Venice) meant that spies were kept busy.

Count Daru in his history of Venice, published at the end of the nineteenth century, produced a very wild document called the 'Statutes of the Inquisitors' which he found in the Royal Library at Paris. This code reads with such a meticulous contempt for the human creature's freedom that it could have been written in the twentieth century. But because of its anachronisms (among them its emphasis on the Spanish embassy) it must be either a deliberate forgery or a document written about the time of the Spanish Plot and therefore not a description of the functions of the Inquisitors as they had been from the beginning. Under these 'Statutes' the Three could punish an offender secretly or publicly as they thought expedient for the state. The stifling *piombi* (cells under the prison roof) and the sodden *pozzi* (at canal level) were at their service. They could draw any amount of money from the treasury of the Ten without explanation. Even the identity of the Inquisitors was not to be revealed. When they decided to release a

B

prisoner after examination, the warder was to fling open his cell-door and shout in the most contemptuous way, 'What are you doing here? Get out!' Spies were to be enticed from every class, and anyone who actually described them as spies was to be arrested and tortured until he confessed how he had arrived at the knowledge. And so it went on, rather like a skit on secret-service machinations. Yet anyone who believes that these 'Statutes' are totally wide of the reality has to remember that the torture inflicted not only on political prisoners but ordinary criminals was sometimes so terrible that they were mutilated for life; they died under the bastinado (the caning of the soles of the feet), the strapado (the flogging of a prisoner strung up by his arms), on the rack, or on the braziers.

The fact was that the governing families could never rely on themselves to keep order. That was why they elected despots, and needed the despotism while hating and fearing it. That was the reason first of all for the Ten and then for the brisker version of the Ten in the Three. Venice gave birth to turbulent, brilliant and heroic men for generation after generation, and her daily problem for over a thousand years was to keep these men from overthrowing the state and exercising personal tyranny with the help of the mob. Social chaos was always a possibility (and one that was fully realised elsewhere in Italy). The aristocracy in the rest of Italy was never a centralised, compact or orderly body: noble families tended to be a law to themselves, so that each principality had a history of endless *coups d'état*. The pattern in France and England was the opposite: there national aristocracies had come about through monarchs who centralised power, above all justice, in their own persons. And Venice achieved something like this orderly pattern of government by a no less hereditary system. She alone in Italy mastered an unruly aristocracy and made a popular rising such a laughable impossibility that only noblemen could have provoked one. There is, however, one clause in the 'Statutes of the Inquisitors' which makes them sound plausible: any patrician found establishing a private tribunal in his own house, whereby an 'enemy' was 'tried' and then punished (quite frequent occurences), was to be put in the Piombi for three years, and drowned on a third conviction; if he 'executed' his victim he was to be executed too.

But no inflexible police state could have lasted even the five hundred years Venice did last after the Closing of the Council, let alone a thousand. Her secret was that her nobles shared not only the fruits of despotism but the discipline as well. Everyone was a victim of what he imposed. The vigilant paring of the doge's power, the trial of heroes soon after their best victories, the illegalisation of snobbery and personal display, was the work of men who were themselves hemmed in with fine rules governing every part of their lives. They had to register their marriages and the birth of their children in the Golden Book within a week, on pain of fines or imprisonment. If they married a woman of the middle classes they were forbidden to register her name or those of their children. It sometimes happened that a man preferred to lose his nobility in exchange for a fat dowry ; and this too the state watched jealously (for fear of losing patricians to a new wealthy class) by limiting a girl's dowry to two thousand ducats unless she was of noble birth.

Being a patrician was a working life. The older men were expected to be present at every council meeting, and there were those who missed hardly a day in thirty and forty years. The Great Council met every day of the week including Sunday and every holiday except 2 March and 31 January (St Mark's Day). In the summer it sat from eight in the morning until noon, in winter from noon to sunset. The senate met Wednesdays and Saturdays; on Saturdays it heard the long, detailed letters from ambassadors abroad. The Spartan machine was so successful that it produced an awed worship even in those who worked it : the higher a man was socially the more awe he felt for the Republic, for his own family name; that was what made him bear torture and imprisonment almost lovingly. Any attention from the Serenissima was better than none.

Chapter 2

'Crafty and Malignant Foxes'

By the beginning of the fifteenth century Venice was at the height of her power. She held much of northern Italy, including Ravenna, Trevisano, Padua, Vicenza, Verona, Crema, Brescia, Bergamo. The bulk of the world's trade was in her hands. She had developed important industries of her own, among them the manufacture of silk, an art brought from Constantinople. She supplied most of the world with it – though it was forbidden to all Venetians except the magistrates as too much of a luxury. Murano glass, another art from the east, supplied the finest mirrors to every capital and palace in Europe. She produced excellent cloth, woven from English and Spanish wool, and her linen was made from Lombardian flax. She produced millions of candles for the Church. Her money was the only currency used by Arabs, Persians, Hindus.

As always she was faced by threats precisely equal to her powers. On her east side the Turks were now strong, because of the weakness of the Byzantine empire (which she more than any other power had caused), and north of the Alps big powers had now come into being, anxious for Italian lands, jealous of her wealth and the long arm of her influence, above all afraid that if uncurbed she would extend her power throughout Europe, with that amazing smooth facility which had made her a legend.

But it was the old Italian enemy, the pope, who brought European jealousy to a head in the League of Cambrai in 1508, usually cited as the beginning of Venice's topple from power. In fact this was the first confederacy of powers in Europe; and it was aimed exclusively against the Republic. In a few months nearly all her territorial possessions had disappeared. Not only was she suddenly dead as a European power but the French began preparing a fleet against her in Genoa.

But it was Venice's magical gift to be never so much on the brink of good fortune as when she seemed quite lost, and vice-versa. Louis XII, having almost got inside her lagoon, unaccountably returned home, and the Cambrai league ended just as it started, in a burst of rage excited by the idea of Venice, but without any practical motive. The French ambassador Louis Hélion raged to Maximilian about her. He felt that 'these Venetians' deserved to be hunted down on sea and land, as people who had 'given up religion'. They were 'crafty and malignant foxes', yet they were also 'proud and ferocious lions'. In the next sentence they were serpents, in the next whales who 'besieged the ocean', more fearful than hurricanes or sea-monsters. And then, to end this menagerie of analogies, he called them 'wolves' and 'tigers' too, and 'souls midway between the Christian and Turk', like 'mischievous goblins'. In his rage the awe is clear to read ; it is turned to hatred by fear – that Venice will overrun the Italian peninsula and make the pope, as he put it, her 'chaplain'.

He went on to list the items of Venetian power: three hundred islands seized from the King of Hungary; two provinces and twelve episcopal cities ; a range of ports along five hundred miles of coast ; conquests in the Byzantine empire, victories over the lords of Padua, Verona, Milan, Ferrara, Mantua, over popes and emperors and kings of Naples. And 'these fishermen' had already agreed among themselves on plans to bridge the Don, the Rhine, the Seine, the Rhône, and to plant their sea-legs in every corner of Europe. And it could have been true.

By 1511 the situation had so changed that the Signory was in alliance with the pope in a Holy League against Louis, whose troops were now causing more alarm to the Church than the Venetians had done. Before two more years had passed Venice was in alliance with Louis, in a treaty which promised the recovery of all her lands. The Signory had learned that when other powers seemed most united against her they were in fact mortally divided. She began to cultivate the art of neutrality, necessarily the key to her foreign policy in the next centuries as her neighbours became stronger and she weaker.

In that long tussle with the European powers in the sixteenth century she lost only Cremona, the land north-west of Cremona along the

Adda, and papal possessions in the Romagna. But it cost her five million ducats. In the worst of the war years she had begun to sell her nobility to raise money for defence ; money could now buy high offices of state, with the result that the quality of the noble class was beginning to go down ; the old trinity of education, courage and birth (though not too much of any of them) as the qualifications of leadership, was gone.

But she might have recovered from this had she been able to clear her vast debt in the old way, by trade. But just as she was irritated by greater powers than herself on land, so she was at sea. Christopher Columbus' discovery of the American lands opened up the necessity of ports on the other side of Europe ; and Vasco de Gama's discovery of the Cape route provided an alternative to the old Venetian line from the east. Commercial importance therefore began to shift to Cadiz and the river Tagus, which took goods straight to the heart of Europe through Spain. The spice cargoes now went direct to Lisbon, and Europeans bought them there instead of in Venice ; Lisbon prices were cheaper than Venetian because the new route avoided Syria and Egypt, where levies (the Turks being in control of Cairo and Alexandria) were imposed on all freight.

It would have been difficult for Venice to switch to the Atlantic trade as her ships were unsuitable for those waters. Protectionism, that bane of failing maritime empires, made things worse: no trade could be done except through Venetian middlemen, and heavy duties were imposed on imports and exports, which brought the ports of Livorno and Genoa into prominence. And protectionism gave a spur to smuggling.

Above all there were now other maritime powers, Britain, Holland and France, to take the place of Venetian galleys in the Mediterranean. Britain was soon to have the most powerful fleet in any sea, and to feel Venetian rivalry so little that she was friendly to her.

These danger-signals were clear to most patricians. They set about reviving agriculture in the areas they still controlled in northern Italy, so as to balance the loss of trade. They fortified Padua and Verona, fearing further German or French attacks. Above all, neutrality was now a crying need: the Republic wanted time to recuperate. Knowing that one false move could unite her enemies against her on land and sea, she played safe for the first time in her history. It was a difficult job chiefly because of the French, who continued to pour down into Italy under François I, thus provoking imperial troops under Charles V, between 1519 and 1523, to do the same. Venice had to vacillate between the two, until luck – in the form of the Turks at the gates of Vienna and religious troubles in Germany – helped her by weakening the emperor. But there were dangers in neutrality. To spur Venice to a closer alliance (that is, military support against the imperial troops) François induced the Sultan to attack her fleet and pillage her islands in the Archipelago.

When the Turks abandoned Cyprus of their own accord Venice celebrated it as her victory: already, in the middle of the sixteenth century, a taste for self-delusion that was to paralyse them two hundred years later was creeping into the people. The neutrality policy began to border on one of capitulation: after a brief alliance with Rome and the emperor against the Turks, the Signory instructed its emissary to talk to the Sultan and propose a tribute of 6,000 ducats for the return of Malvasia and Napoli di Romagna, plus 300,000 ducats as indemnity for the late war, and should the Sultan turn it down the emissary was to cede these two towns anyway – in other words, get peace at any price. The Sultan not only turned it down with great ferocity and insisted on the cession of the two towns, but asked for some of Venice's posts in Dalmatia as well, plus the 300,000 ducats. The remarkable thing is that the Signory accepted: they only found out afterwards that their instructions to the emissary had been previously leaked to the Sultan by one of their own secretaries of the Ten.

Venice's love of grand spectacle reached its height at this time. For the wedding between the reigning doge Lorenzo Priuli and Zilia Dandolo on 18 September 1557, tapestries were hung everywhere, triumphal arches constructed at every corner. With regattas, fireworks, balls lasting until dawn, the party went on for three whole days – in every part of the city; the crowds were so thick round the Basilica doors that the ceremony could not be heard inside. It was a hundred years since the people had had a dogaressa. That was the kind of political event that moved people now.

Three *provveditori delle pompe* or 'supervisors of luxury' were made part of the constitution to administer those Sumptuary Laws that had already been passed without effect. Every aspect of dress – the amount of material used for sleeves, the decorations on shoes – was officially overseered. *Avvogadori* were technically able to stop you in the street and measure you up, though it only happened once or twice in a century. A decree limited the number of dinner parties a patrician in high office could give to his relatives to two a month, and he could have no more than ten guests at a time. For weddings he was allowed forty guests only, one dish of roast meats and one dish of boiled (and in neither dish was there to be more than three kinds of meat). At dinner-parties of more than twenty guests no oysters could be eaten. Inspectors could sniff round your kitchen and dining room at any time.

Women could wear only one colour, whether of velvet, damask or satin; only in the case of Persian silks and brocades were different colours allowed, but then these could have no trimming. The feathers of a fan were not to be worth more than four ducats. No low-necked dresses were allowed, presumably because the bare skin was a field for lavish necklaces. Only the *dozete* (the doge's daughters and grand-daughters) were exempted from these laws, together with the dogaressa. A belt sparkling with fine pearls and thirty gold rosettes which the Duke of Savoy gave to the wife of Luigi Mocenigo during the state visit of Henri III of France in 1574 had to be handed over to the *provveditori*, who then decided on what state occasions the lady might wear it.

Of all symbols of wealth the gondola was the most closely watched. It had always been a special mark of the patrician class, and probably derived not from the ordinary Venetian transport boat but the smoother and more elegant caïque of the Bosphorus, which still bore the steel 'beak' or toothed decoration of the ancient Roman galley. At first a frame was mounted mid-boats, and hoods thrown over it to make a cabin: then, as the taste for comfort and luxury grew, the more elaborate *felze* with their carpets and curtains came into being.

....

From Venetian windows
OPPOSITE Watching a procession
OVERLEAF A canal by the stonemason's yard

In the sixteenth century there were over ten thousand gondolas in Venice, and every article displayed on them came within the scope of meticulous laws stipulating what material the hoods must be made of, what cushions and carpets could be used, the number of gold or brass fittings, the number of gondoliers. A strict decree of 1562 brought the present funereal-looking boat into being. Only foreign ambassadors and the doge could decorate their gondolas as they pleased. A glance at Canaletto's *Reception for the Ambassador Bolagno* (in the Crespi Collection in Milan) will show us to what exuberant lengths this could go, in carved and gilded putti and sea-figures, rosettes and crowns and flourished cornices. But then the foreign embassies competed with each other in show. And that was just what the Ten wanted to avoid among Venetians, knowing that it could have brought the state down.

Venice was more splendid to the eye than ever, though not so intimately ravishing. Palaces in an opulently proud style began to fill the banks of the Grand Canal. Together with the luxury, and greater attention to holidays, the size of the population was going down. The banking system faltered and many of the patrician families were ruined. The young men of these ruined families became intriguers, the material for espionage, hanging about the Broglio for news. This in turn bolstered the remaining wealthy families and made distinctions of class a fact, however little this was desired or promoted. Here was the social situation that made 'supervisors of luxury' necessary – lavish showing-off against a background of envy.

At the end of the sixteenth century an ineffectual decree of banishment was issued against the hordes of *bravi* or hired assassins in the city. They were the end-result of the atmosphere of mistrust that the oligarchy's elaborate system of espionage had started. They came from every part of Europe and often took refuge in the foreign embassies, jeering at the pursuing *sbirri*, or constables, from the windows. All this meant a state of turmoil – hidden by astonishing opulence.

The fact that there was order at all was due to the cruellest features of the government ; but these at the same time produced the disorder. Just as Venice became a resort of pleasure, so it provided a refuge for adventurers and social misfits from every part of Europe. And these

Woman on a balcony

made up the armies of *bravi*. The historian Romanin drew up a list of the secret drownings that took place between 1551 and 1604: most years they amount to only a handful, but in 1559 and 1560, and then in the last years of the century, they show a sudden increase, reflecting the state of nervousness in political quarters. The so-called *signorotti* on the mainland – Venetian landlords not inscribed in the Golden Book but rich enough to hire *bravi* – caused a lot of trouble, mostly for the pleasure of it. They were executed when caught, but were hardened to the threat of execution. The power of chivalry had ceased. In fact, excess and criminality began to take on a chivalrous aspect. As a remedy against the *bravi* the Ten joined them, so to speak: they invited them to murder each other; the murderer of a *bravo* received full pardon. A patrician who killed one of Titian's servants absolved himself in this way by also killing a *bravo*. But the remedy soon had to be discontinued, since you could define any personal enemy as a *bravo*.

Henri III's reception in July 1574, when he passed through the city on his way back from Poland to take up the French crown, surpassed anything known before. The Sumptuary Laws were suspended for ten days. Forty of the best-looking sons of great houses attended the king as pages. At the landing of S. Nicolò the triumphal arch, designed by Palladio, was covered with ten pictures by Tintoretto and Veronese. A vast awning was thrown across St Mark's Square, painted with stars; splendid carpets were spread on the pavement. The sea-pageants were more extravagant than ever before; boats were decorated with fabulous tapestries and silks and brocades; sea-monsters made of Murano glass belched smoke and flames from furnaces inside. There was a banquet of welcome for three thousand guests, and the various dishes numbered twelve hundred in all; everything was served on silver plate. The king sat under a golden canopy. He is said to have dreamed of returning for the rest of his life.

The Signory's objective here was to secure French friendship: almost unknown to themselves they were changing their methods of diplomacy; policy was no longer based squarely on power but on an

....

expense-account that would soon prove ruinous, in an atmosphere of allurement.

The period of repose was broken by the fact that the new Sultan wanted Cyprus, which had slept in Venetian arms since the middle of the fifteenth century. Selim II even told the Signory that he wanted it. Again a desperate search for funds went on. High offices of state were again on sale: for 20,000 ducats you could even become a Procurator of St Mark, the second highest dignity in the state; patrician youths could buy their way into the Great Council for a lower price than ever before.

Cyprus was lost but Venice was happy enough not to be invaded herself. Then something happened that seemed to renew the possibility even of invasion. This was the so-called Spanish Plot in 1618 which, according to Henry Wotton, the English ambassador there, plunged the city into 'horror and confusion'. Between three and five hundred men were strangled in prison, drowned in the silence of the night, hanged in public view, in the course of two or three days. And no one, including most of the Venetian noblemen, seemed to know what it was all about.

For over three decades now the Spanish had been established in Milan, Naples and Palermo, governing through viceroys. Their Inquisition made Rome's look benevolent; their taxes throttled the initiative of the peoples under them. Spanish money poured into Venice to corrupt those patricians who needed it badly enough. Thus a Spanish Plot was never out of the question. Henry Wotton thought it was a French conspiracy, and the people – to judge by the way they stormed the Spanish embassy – thought it was a Spanish one. Count Daru's explanation (by far the most interesting) is that it was neither. He holds that the Venetian Inquisitors watched the situation for quite ten months before they did anything. The plot was revealed to them by a French agent called Jacques Pierre, who had been in the Duke of Osuna's hire and had fled to Venice. His story, according to the official account put out by the Ten, was that the Duke of Osuna was plotting the overthrow of Venice. But Daru's clever analysis is that the Signory knew all about the duke's design, which was actually to overthrow Spanish rule in Naples with the help of Venice, under the cover of a plot against her. Spain suddenly found out and it became necessary to wipe out all trace of the Ten's part in the deal. In a matter of days every conspirator was removed.

Whatever the explanation of those corpses swinging between the columns on the Piazzetta, they made people more fearfully aware than ever before of the power of the Ten. The Spanish Plot was the climax of a Venetian process towards absolute power which had been going on for at least four centuries. The system of espionage had become such a natural form of government that it was like a separate ministry whose functionaries had a common interest in keeping their work going. Spies clubbed together and chose noblemen to work against in frame-ups that rarely failed. Not five years after the Spanish Plot a senator and *cavaliere* called Antonio Foscarini, one-time ambassador in London, was chosen for one of these operations. As to whether it was the spies' private decision to single him out, or some enmity on the part of the Ten, or a Jesuit machination, no one will ever know. But he was accused of going to the (now hated) Spanish embassy after dark in disguise. After a few secret examinations he was strangled in his dungeon. Less than a year later the Ten issued a decree absolving him from all guilt, after the spies had been executed. We must remember that by now the Ten were ten different men from six months before: the faction had changed. Those with a grievance against the loudly eccentric Foscarini might have gone, and a Foscarini faction taken their place. That was how Venetian politics worked.

At this period, late in Venice's history, we should not look for the collusion and compact identity of interest between the ruling patricians that we find earlier. Despotism was useless in the hands of people not agreed among themselves. In 1625 Reniero Zeno, one of the chiefs of the Ten, managed to deprive the doge's son of his seat in the Great Council, for which slight the son's *bravi* stabbed him almost to death. After the son's very light sentence of banishment to Ferrara, Zeno tried to question the doge's integrity. But this time he failed to carry the Ten with him, and when he tried to stage a mild palace-revolt the Inquisitors gave him ten years' imprisonment.

Zeno's friends then refused to tender enough votes to make a further
Ten possible. A committee was set up to look into the Ten's activities, and a decree was carried that the Ten should no longer be qualified
to interfere with the Great Council's legislation ; in an angry debate
the sentence against Zeno was annulled. The despotism was thus on the
brink of disbanding itself. But there was a sudden warning voice as to
what this might mean : government once thrown open to anyone would
become the province of everyone ; the oligarchy would collapse. That
voice was Battista Nani's ; he saved the state just in time to face another war with the Turks.

Really the war for Crete (or Candia) went on for the next twenty-
four years in a series of campaigns so murderous that for at least two
centuries afterwards the Venetians called a war to the knife *una vera
guerra di Candia*, 'a real Candian war'. Once again Venice had to do
the impossible and float loans out of proportion to her resources. The
price of war far exceeded the five million ducats coming in annually
from taxation (*essere in Candia* meant 'penniless'). Every Venetian had
to give up three-quarters of his family plate to the state for melting
down ; again the highest offices were put up for sale ; any man able to
pay the upkeep of a thousand soldiers for a whole year, and put down
sixty thousand ducats towards that expenditure in cash, could become
a nobleman.

Venice won victory after victory but without changing the situation.
Once, in 1654, eight Venetian galleys defended themselves in the Dar-
danelles against many times their number, and later in the same place
forty galleys put a hundred Turkish boats to flight, and burned eighty-
five of them. This was in the old tradition. The senate was even
traditional enough to retain its old grudge towards its popular heroes,
and Lazaro Mocenigo, being the natural choice for commander-in-chief
after the death of Marcello, was passed over for another man. But
times had changed : the Great Council countermanded the order. And
when Francesco Morosini was called before the Ten some years later
after a disappointing campaign in which fifteen hundred of his men had
been killed and almost all his seamen had died of scurvy, there was a
difference here too : he was acquitted, and not because of philanthropy

so much as a shrewd conviction that heroes these days were harder to come by. Morosini had charge of Crete in the final siege: in the first six months alone seventeen sorties and thirty-two assaults were launched against him. With fewer than three thousand men left he sued for peace. The fall of Crete in 1669, and not anything decided by Napoleon over a century later, was the real end of the Republic. From this time on, Venice simply enjoyed herself. And the whole of Europe flocked down to see her do it.

Chapter 3

The Aristocratic
Showcase of Europe

Eighteenth-century Venice looked a picture of triumph, as if she had never had a defeat and her empire was everlasting. She even seemed on the same level as the other powers of Europe. And in a most un- canny way she was. Her stores of secret diplomatic knowledge, her political wiles learned over the centuries, her instinctively sound judge- ments kept her prestige intact. Between 1700 and 1797 she lost hardly a yard of territory. Her two million colonial subjects, dispersed on islands and forts all the way down the Adriatic to the Aegean, led peacefully decaying lives. The *ancien régime* everywhere needed her, had a vested interest in her survival as the aristocratic showcase of Europe where revolution was thought an impossibility.

As a result of this tacit protection she began to feel a real security for the first time in her history. A vast sigh of relief seemed to go through every class. At last she could sit back and enjoy herself. Every prince in Europe admired her, politics aside. Above all she was so old that no one seriously believed she could ever die. She had survived so much. Yet this last period of survival was different: she had become a tourist attraction.

And with this her will to be independent began to die. The more tourists, the more rotten her aristocracy. She no longer had to fight, for the simple reason that no one was likely to plunder her any more. So her constitution was no longer needed, with its method of investing man with emergency powers while vigilantly and petulantly curbing that power.

Safety was the distinctive quality of eighteenth-century Venice. She became a grand drawing room where the faces were familiar, and intrigue was in the air ; every habit had the legendary power of a ritual in this drawing room, as predictable as the rising of the sun. Goldoni's plays again and again evoke this drawing room in the full swing of its social life, the sun glittering through its windows, the walls shimmering with reflected light from the canal outside. Venice was much like an island now, as remote from armed frontiers as England, almost as free, now that politics and religion (hitherto forbidden subjects of conversation) were as frivolous as a game of cards – more so, since less depended on them.

The rude, festivity-hating husbands of Goldoni's *I Rusteghi*, whose wives dress lavishly half to spite them, whose children rebel against them graciously, are the last, now grotesque, echoes of the sixteenth century: grotesque because these merchants would look ridiculous with a sword. They hate a play or an opera, forbid their women to wear masks; they invest their money soundly and spend it on the best food and wine, on furniture and efficient servants; their homes are little citadels grimly shut to the outside world; even their close relatives are unwelcome. Yet the masked Venice outside permeates the shuttered houses; every day it bustles, like the beginning of a grand fête. And the 'barbarians', as Goldoni calls these husbands, have to give in. They threaten to beat their wives, but are frightened of getting a beating themselves. Violence is out of the question in this world. It is all so harmless, intimate, happy, as long as you don't think too much. Even the daughter kept prisoner all day, forbidden to look over her balcony, let alone see the youth chosen to marry her, shines with the happiness only intimacy gives. Peeping over the balcony means peeping into another drawing room: one drawing room gives place to another, until they reach their glowing climax in the Piazza, where the 'barbarians' never once take their children.

The Piazza of the *cafés* came into being in these last hundred years of independence. No casino of importance was far from it. The things decided on the Broglio were no longer high policy or a secret assassination but a love-affair, a loan, a marriage. For nearly a hundred years Venice had virtually no politics of her own.

But reading *I Rusteghi* we cannot doubt that something new was at work in Venetian life, deliberate and conscious, quite unlike anything that had gone before, and not designed just for pleasure. It was a

will to soften and civilise life outside the small area of the noble class ;
their manners, now sweet and ingratiating where they had once been
stern, percolated down to the other classes as an ideal of life. Noblemen had given up fighting (even each other), and their benevolence was
now democratic, bestowed even on foreigners. The best-dressed wife
of one of the *rusteghi* scolds the four husbands to take a gentler, more
open attitude not only to close relatives, but to other Venetians, even
'foreigners' (meaning Italians from outside Venice). And she wins on
all her points. The ideal is no longer the tyrannical, unflinching, heroic
manner of the great past. In her the new Venice is talking.

The little city in the sea still lived in the old régime, like all of Italy,
but she was far beyond the rest of Italy in her powers of social development. She liquidated her noble class, now that its function was over,
far more effectively than the French did at the end of the same century, and without bloodshed ; social contrasts simply faded away in the
light, misty colours of her drawing rooms. The danger of revolution
in Venice, though it caused a lot of alarm among her richer noblemen
at the end of the century, was absurdly slight because of her highly
evolved society, with its harmonious methods of change. Perhaps no
noble class in eighteenth-century Europe was easier for a counterfeit
nobleman to enter, simply because 'noble' had come to mean a manner,
which anyone could imitate. And what the pretty, masked wife does in
I Rusteghi is to invite these rich 'barbarians' to be noblemen, not boors
any more.

There was no more aristocratic city in Europe and yet there was
complete familiarity between the different classes. Servants lost their
tempers with masters. It was money that counted in this Venice. The
marquis in Goldoni's *La Locandiera* offers the pretty innkeeper his
'protection', in exchange for which he expects a bit of love. But noble
protection, once a powerful shield for people of the lower classes,
is now a sham and a name, and she says so. The count who gives her
jewels has that much more sway over her. The marquis's sword, when
someone pulls it out of its sheath in anger, turns out to be broken off
at the hilt; he asks the knight to be careful with it – 'that hilt cost

c

money!' That was the extent to which a serious noble class had ceased to exist.

But all western Europe had become civil by the eighteenth century. Chivalry, which had started as a medieval dream to make life more gentle, was now achieved in daily habits. Wars were milder than ever before. Since the middle of the seventeenth century much of the old barbarity had gone out of battle. Pillaging and looting were replaced by fixed levies. The peasants and farmers ceased to suffer as before ; Adam Smith said that the farmers of the Netherlands now got rich in war by paying no rents and selling produce at wild prices. Many more prisoners were taken these days; there were fewer casualties. Compared with the Thirty Years War, the War of the Spanish Succession in the 1730s was a series of manoeuvres. Battle became an accepted part of social life. Wives travelled with their officer-husbands, and battle was so harmless that during lulls the officers' quarters, where every gaiety took place, often led straight out on to the battlements. Commanders tended to avoid a striking victory because it obliged them to defend large areas, which then created problems of supply, and in any case victory threatened their livelihood by shortening the war. The armies were still mercenary – German, Swedish, Russian soldiers – under the command of noblemen and those few bourgeois who could purchase commissions. The idea that an army could be composed of one's own citizens, even one's own peasantry, thus robbing society of its means of livelihood, was thought thoroughly barbarous (it was advanced by Machiavelli) ; only Russia, Spain and Prussia had a form of even mild conscription.

Italy, as always, was the major battlefield. But it was all as orderly and chivalrous as a Grand Tour. There was a polite re-shuffle of Italian possessions. Austria exchanged Sicily for Sardinia with the Duke of Savoy. The War of the Polish Succession brought Don Carlos the Bourbon down to Naples, where he threw out the Austrians and established the Kingdom of the Two Sicilies. Seven years later Tuscany went to Francis of Lorraine, by right ; he had just married Maria Theresa, putting Tuscany under the Austrian house. Thus the Bourbons held the south of Italy, and the Hapsburgs, with a viceroy in Milan and a grand duke in Tuscany, the north. That was the Italian picture for most of the eighteenth century. And the two armies, the Bourbon and the Hapsburg, engaged in courtly, sporadic warfare on principles perfectly understood between them. Italy was not so much a country invaded and ruled by foreigners, as a land of the past necessarily governed by foreigners because they were up-to-date. Venice, Rome and Savoy stood aloof from this occupied Italy, but their independence was, so to speak, hardly necessary now because the same sort of life went on everywhere. And no one was going to harm them, in this delightful playground of the Grand Tour.

In fact, the meaning of the word 'foreign' had changed. Everyone of importance now spoke French. The noblemen of Europe had more in common with each other than with their own peasants. Venice no longer had a watchful, hostile world at her doorstep. The doge Manin, who handed her over to Napoleon at the end of the century, was probably closer to him than to his own people, in whom he saw 'revolution'. This identity of interest and feeling came about during the eighteenth century: Europe was a whole civilisation for the first time.

Naturally Venice was its jewel. And even she was mild now; there is the famous story that the poison used by the Inquisitors was found to have congealed, and the recipe for it lost. The atmosphere of dangerous intrigue was still there, but like a ghost. It gave the enchantment of the city a touch almost of depravity, for those with imaginations. And the stories of secret drownings – sacks thrown into canals – were like the tales of kings; they had something grand about them, the shudder they provoked was a pleasure. When he was warned that he was being watched by government agents Montesquieu burned the notes he'd made on the Inquisitors, packed his bags and rushed off to Holland. But it was a practical joke.

Nowhere were people better trained for a good time. Casanova's memoirs read like an account of expert strategy across endless terrains of pleasure, in Venice, Paris, Vienna, London. It was perfectly put in his casual '*Je sortis pour vaguer à mes affaires, c'est à dire à mes plaisirs.*'

The energy devoted to pleasure could have run a dozen other cities.

As a visiting Frenchman said, 'No one gets dressed here until people are going to bed elsewhere.' Pleasure was the medicine that deferred old age: 'No one here,' according to Lady Mary Wortley Montagu, 'is old as long as he is not bedridden.' This pleasure-hunt was a display of powers, a search for the *tour de force* in everything. In the artists it brimmed over. Gianbattista Tiepolo painted twelve apostles half life-size in ten hours, just for a wager: the subject – not to say the sacredness of the subject – had nothing to do with it. In the brilliance of that painter's light, like the sky splitting open, there is the celebration of artistic energy as an end in itself. He displays the most stunning skill. Nothing to do with the brush is beyond him. He is said to have taken less time to produce a picture than others took to grind their colours.

The bankers and business men failed to influence life as they did in other European capitals, where they brought clear prose and good sense. They succumbed, like the *rusteghi*, to the endless masquerade round them. No Venetian was interested in Isaac Newton, even if he remembered Galileo. The idea of a symmetrical universe working under laws as clear and regular as Pope's couplets had little fascination for people more or less brought up on nature as Arcadia (especially as they had no green nature of their own to speak of). Venetians played at all ideas except Newtonian and Kantian ones. Their noblemen, especially the disgruntled and penniless 'Barnabotti', read Voltaire and Helvétius partly because Paris was fashionable and partly because these authors attacked the Church. Since no idea was really in earnest – only carried like a feather in the hat – there could be no religion. Everybody 'believed' as a matter of social decorum. Clairvoyance, the horoscope, fortune-telling, and 'science' (a muddle of astounding parlour-tricks), not only fascinated people but made money. Casanova's most profitable pose was that of a cabalist, which got him an income, a gondola, servants and a large apartment in the Grimani palace before he was thirty. The Church in Venice was simply an aspect of that city's ecstatic worldliness, and nearly every Mass was a brilliant concert, a performance in every sense.

It was the age of the *tour de force* for Venice – in love intrigues, music, painting, the theatre. She sent architects, painters, musicians to every part of Europe ; great houses fought over them. Her Murano glass, her lacework, her cloth of gold (which alone brought in twelve million sequins a year) were famous everywhere. She was a tiny stage now, filled with talents drawn from a long, rich, disciplined past. Her taste was towards the small and detailed – the miniature portrait, the detailed *veduta* as opposed to the grand canvas, the sonnet instead of the epic, the comedy (its touch necessarily deft and light, however deep the satire bit) rather than the tragedy. During the whole century only one real tragedy was tried in the Venetian theatre, and it was an immediate howling flop. Any grand enterprise was definitely unfashionable. The heroic verged on the laughable. There was a feeling that if anything big was to be done, anything striking and new, unless it was an *aria* or a clever bit of asymmetry in a stucco ceiling, it should be in the hands of foreigners. A man with something new in his head failed to get on in Venice. As for the old kind of patriotism, it too had become miniature, at best provincial pride.

But, far from drawing in her horns now that her empire was stagnant and foreigners controlled the plains of Lombardy, she spent more than ever before. In 1703 Venice was still earning about ten million ducats annually from marine insurance ; her taxes were higher than they had ever been. Some of her riches might have been spent on her outposts in the Aegean, or in laying the basis of a land-army. Instead she spent stupendous sums on the yearly Ascension Day celebrations. In 1732 the elections of the doge cost four times what they had in the most prosperous epochs before. Thirty years after that they were even double that figure. In a word, Venice was living on her capital.

Yes everything *seemed* positive – people's manners, the two hundred cafés many of which were open all night, the domino that hid all sign of class in a new democracy of pleasure, the convents where noble women held salons and marriages were arranged, the 'triangle' of the husband, wife and *cicisbeo* (male chaperone). There was an open attitude to all things on one condition – that the serious, the original, the expansionist, above all the heroic, were avoided. *There* the good will suddenly ceased, and the old implacable Venetian was alive again. There was a morbid side to his taste for the light and gracious and outwardly successful ; it went too far to be quite healthy. Once when a young couple committed suicide handkerchiefs were sold with a death's head embroidered in one corner and the initials of the lovers in the other, inside a garland of drops of blood.

While in 1645 there had been well over two thousand workers at the Arsenal, there were under fifteen hundred by the year 1766, and according to the Frenchman de Brosses, even these seemed to do no work : the job was now a sinecure. In 1581 the nobility had formed nearly five per cent (about two thousand families) of the whole population, whereas in 1766 they were well under three per cent (about a thousand families). Between 1627 and 1788 one hundred and seven new families were added to the nobility, so that in fact the old class had decreased even more. In the midst of the lavish spending (with wealth concentrated in fewer and fewer families) there was more misery in the lowest classes than before : the infantile mortality rate rose steeply during the century. The population of Livorno went up seven times in the same period. At the end of the sixteenth century Venice had had close on one hundred and fifty thousand inhabitants, but by the end of the eighteenth century there were only one hundred and thirty-seven thousand.

Yet the Venetian navy was still an amazing force, at least at the beginning of the century – quick, unhesitating, despite the fact that it consisted mostly of unwieldy vessels from the merchant marine. Angelo Emo's bombardment of Susa, Tunis and Bizerta in the sixties of the previous century had been proof that her artillery too was modern and effective. But from that point on there was no development. Her armaments began to show poor design because her will to war had ceased ; her neutrality, which became a frantic principle of government during her last years, was at bottom not a political decision at all but weak procrastination. Many of her possessions – like Crete and Cyprus – were lost unnecessarily. Service in the navy, which had always been compulsory (a nobleman was expected to have had two years at sea before he took up his place in the Great Council), was now paid for like any other job. There were endless frauds in the Arsenal, and orders for new supplies were hopelessly delayed. The seamen showed less discipline than ever before. The specially appointed 'Inquisition of the Arsenal' tried to make reforms, but this was an old office in origin, and it failed to make an urgent new approach. The English and Dutch navies were now manifestly superior in discipline, sea-worthiness and armament, apart from strategy.

State expenditure was kept down to a minimum, but outposts were expensive even at their present level of stagnation ; and there was all the old machinery of international diplomacy which cost money with-out serving any purpose. The highest city magistrates were poorly paid, compared with those of Paris and London. The national debt reached eighty million ducats at the beginning of the century, obliging the state to pay an annual interest of two and a half million, though peace reduced this figure in the next eighty years. But Venice was too lovely to care.

Charles de Brosses, travelling earlier in the century, came up the Brenta from Padua in a boat called *Il Bucentoro* but in fact a 'very small child' of the real thing, its cabin hung in brocade, with leather-covered tables and little windows and glass doors. But he was un-moved by his first sight of the city. He thought the entrance to the Grand Canal much like that to Lyons or Paris by river. But once there, among palaces that seemed to grow out of the water, he was so astonished that he never really recovered from it. This man, president of the Burgundy parliament, moved among ambassadors, and every patrician pleasure was open to him. 'Nothing can equal the liberty that exists and the tranquillity that one enjoys,' he wrote, 'so much so that I regard it as the securest town in Europe.'

....

Chapter 4

Bread and Circuses

Venice's pomp, which had started in the tradition of Juvenal's bread and circuses, to flatter a people with no voice in politics, now became a sort of self-advertisement. Though Negropont, Cyprus and Crete, the basis of her empire, were lost, their full armorial bearings could still be seen on the three flags that fluttered from St Mark's on holidays. It was appearance that counted in the eighteenth century.

She seemed to be drifting into a narrow intimacy, rich because of the past and determined more and more by hardly conscious customs no one could remember the origin of. These, not problems of survival, were now the sacred things.

The women's fashion of high clogs that had reached its climax in the previous century showed how Venice loved its eccentricities. It had made the foreigners gape. Whenever noblewomen walked out of doors or stepped into their gondolas they were impeded by what John Evelyn called 'great scaffolds': they stood half as tall again as passers-by, and leaned on the heads of two serving women. The habit had originated in the fourteenth century as a protection against mud, but gradually, when the taste for display started, the height of the clogs grew. Some said it was a shrewd way of keeping the women in order, by making quick movement impossible. But perhaps more than anything it sprang from an increasing desire to make life a masquerade, with the patricians as the masters of ceremony.

It was the same with the domino, which more and more gripped the Venetian imagination, until it was the accepted wear not only of the patricians at carnival time but the common people as well, in annulment of class. These fashions separated Venice from the rest of the world with something like oriental inscrutability. She began to seem unreal as if, now that her power was in decline, the sea had crept in

....

The city on the water
OPPOSITE Gondolas by the Piazzetta
OVERLEAF A regatta on the Grand Canal

with its everlasting mists, its ravishing sunlit days, and taken hold of the physical city, drawn it into something like a dream, from which the inhabitants would never recover. The gently suicidal enticements which people have noticed there – and run away from – began before the seventeenth century was out. Thomas Mann's Venice, where love has become a plague, originates then.

The women wore their hair long, streaked with various colours, an effect which they prepared for hours on end, combing it through a wide crownless hat in the sunlight of their *altine* or terraces. Their petticoats hung straight from their arm-pits, 'all apron', as John Evelyn put it, with wide sleeves that showed bare arms under veils of tiffany. Their shoulders were covered with an almost transparent yellow lawn. The middle-class women and the courtesans wore veils of taffeta or glossy silk over their heads and shoulders, peeping out now and again.

A procession through the streets was still enough to convince the people, and perhaps some nobles, that the old power was still there. The most lavish welcomes in Europe were still given to foreign princes – the old recipe of fireworks, acrobatics, regattas on the Grand Canal, fisticuffs between the Nicolotti and the Castellani. One German prince was so stupefied by it that he tried to escape. There was so much pleasure to be had, for at least six months of the year, during the carnival, that the vast palaces on either side of the Grand Canal, built in the serious past, seemed too gloomy now. Not only the common people but the nobles lived *in piazza*.

Anything was an excuse for a party – the return of prisoners-of-war from Turkey, a military victory of no great worth, the arrival of a foreign ambassador. People poured through the narrow *calle*, the bells rang, the shop-shutters were pulled down. The festival of the *Salute* and that of the *Redentore* were thanksgiving celebrations for Venice's delivery from the plagues of 1576 and 1630: people ate suppers on boats in the Grand Canal, the gardens of the Giudecca were crowded with booths and pavilions hung with fairy lights, a bridge of boats was made from the church of the *Salute* (or *Redentore*) to the other side of the Canal, and at dawn everyone went to the Lido to see the

....

Boatmen on the lagoon

sun rise. The high spots of the year, when the doge went in procession, were Corpus Christi, Good Friday and Easter.

Frederick IV, King of Denmark and Norway, visited the city in 1708 and stayed for three months of regattas, processions, church functions, and balls, suppers and concerts at the Dolfin, Nani and Morosini palaces. The same happened to Frederick Christian, son of the King of Poland, when he came about thirty years later. In 1755 Duke Clement Augustus of Bavaria was served on gold plate at a table shaped like a horse-shoe, before one hundred and eighty guests; the dessert was a special design by Marco Franceschi and had thirty-five centre dishes and forty-eight side dishes of various syrups, without mentioning the fruit ices served on thirty-two silver salvers; the palace (Palazzo Nani on the Giudecca) was lit outside by forty-four torches. Vast honours were bestowed on Edward Augustus, Duke of York, and he saw the finest regatta of the century: there were two balls, the first given by him at the Ca' Rezzonico, the other a state occasion where the women were so covered with pearls and precious stones that, according to one guest, 'you could have taken them for Sultans'. The Duke of Würtemberg, Charles Eugene, came in 1767 and hired three palaces for himself and his suite of seventy-five musicians, servants and courtiers. The son of the doge Mocenigo gave a concert for him in the cloisters of the Mendicanti which started at two o'clock in the morning and ended at five, with unmonastic lashings of food and drink all the time. Only one great celebrity escaped the Venetian net of delights, and that was the Emperor Joseph II who visited the city incognito in 1769 and asked for solitude so that he could see the sights. But he did have two parties, one at the Ca' Rezzonico and the other at the Tron house. Even a pope visited Venice in the eighteenth century, so harmless was the atmosphere of Italian politics: he was met by the doge near S. Giorgio and taken in the golden *Bucentoro*, or ship of state, to the monastery of Ss. Giovanni e Paolo; the choirmaster Pasquale Galuppi gave his cantata for five voices, *The Return of Tobias* (words by Gasparo Gozzi), though the pope, keeping up Rome's long philistine tradition, was not present.

The sovereign to whom Venice gave most of her all was the Grand

Duke of Russia, Paul Petrovitch, in 1782. He and his wife travelled under the names 'Counts of the North'; their entrance from Mestre to Venice was followed by state gondolas and splendidly decorated boats, while crowds waited at the Rialto. That evening they were received by two hundred flunkies in liveries of gold and velvet; a ball was given at the Teatro S. Benedetto where the boxes were made out as complete boudoirs with pillars and ceilings of gilded papier-mâché, while the stage was hung with huge Murano mirrors, the auditorium with blue silver-fringed drapes of silk. After a regatta there was a procession called 'The Triumph of Peace' inside a vast arena specially set up in the Piazza, its boxes as high as the columns of the Procuratie: the Goddess of Peace sat in a massive carriage with Abundance crowning her with olive branches, while Mars and Bellona lay before her throne; and the carriage – like the four preceding hers – was drawn by pure-white oxen.

Two years later attention was switched to perhaps Russia's bitterest enemy, Sweden, when King Gustavus III paid a visit during the Ascension Day celebrations. On his second evening the Palazzo Pisani was lit simultaneously with torches outside and chandeliers inside, its windows thrown open. There were eight hundred guests at supper, with gold plate at the royal table. Three days later the Pisanis gave a reception at their pleasure-house on the Giudecca; imitation fruit of crystal with fluttering candles inside hung from the trees; masses of flowers were cut for the rooms. Twelve days of this made the king ill; the Pisanis spent over one hundred thousand lire on their two parties – the kind of money that could have kept a family for a lifetime.

Yet Venice was not wholly comfortable for foreigners, unless they were diplomats or princes. The beggars were 'saucy and airy and odd in their manners', according to Mrs Thrale; they invaded the city at Ascension time and their horrible deformities could be seen everywhere. Like the piles of filth in the *calle* and floating on the canals, they were gently tolerated. Mrs Thrale noticed that the beggars were treated with the greatest softness by all classes. Her friends treated her maid with affection and kindliness, and called her 'sorella'. She felt harsh next to them. Yet she writes that the Rialto bridge is 'so dirtily kept and deformed with mean shops that, passing over it, disgust gets the better of every other sensation ... St Mark's Place is all covered over in a morning with chicken-coops, which stink one to death, as nobody, I believe, thinks of changing their baskets ; and all about the ducal palace is made so very offensive by the resort of human creatures for every purpose most unworthy of so charming a place, that all enjoyment of its beauties is rendered difficult to a person of any delicacy, and poisoned so provokingly, that I do never cease to wonder that so little police and proper regulation are established in a city so particularly lovely to render her sweet and wholesome.'

William Beckford, the young English millionaire, bore her out: 'One circumstance alone prevents my observing half the treasures of the place, and holds down my fancy just springing into the air: I mean the vile stench which exhales from every recess and corner of the edifice, and which all the incense of the altars cannot subdue. When no longer able to endure this noxious atmosphere, I run up the Campanile in the piazza, and seating myself amongst the pillars of the gallery, breathe the fresh gales which blow from the Adriatic.' That and the beggars and cripples ('unfit to be surveyed by any eyes except those of the surgeon') were the only things that made Mrs Thrale's departure easy : otherwise she would have broken her heart to leave 'people who show such tenderness towards their friends'. Her friend Bragadin promised her (with almost eastern charm) that when she came back she should walk about the town in white satin slippers and never see a beggar from one end of Venice to the other. Or was he being ironical ?

As processions satisfied the appetite for spectacle, gambling took the place of risk, now that there was so little of it in Venetian life. Everybody played. The obsession cut through all classes ; and the government was in continuous alarm about it. In 1638 the Ten had decided to ride with the growing mania rather than, by opposing it, increase the risk and therefore the pleasure. They approved a public gaming house at the theatre of S. Moisè, part of Marco Dandolo's house, in the annex or *ridotto*, where the audience usually gathered during the intervals. The opera house and the *ridotto* really developed side by side, and

sprang from much the same need for relaxing society. Even contacts
with foreigners were made possible by these *ridotti*, where card tables
were set up and refreshments could be had, behind the boxes. The
foyer of the S. Moisè *ridotto* was hung with stamped leather ; two rooms
led off, one for chocolate, tea or coffee and the other for sausages,
fruit, cheese, wine ; and beyond these were ten saloons, where the
games were played – *faraone, biribisso, pichèto, panfil, bassetta, sette
e mezzo, maccà, cresciman.*

At each table a patrician held the bank, with piles of sequins and
ducats before him ; to play you either had to be a patrician, and wear
your official cloak, or sport a mask : the patricians were allowed to
unmask whenever they wanted, and there was no bar to women. In
fact, gambling obsessed the women far more than scandal or love affairs.
The stakes were high. Playing began between eight and ten in the
morning, according to the time of year. The women sometimes lost
family fortunes and sold what was left of their virtue in order to do the
same again next evening. The usurer's trade naturally thrived, and
not only patricians but common people were at their mercy. The
number of players at the S. Moisè *ridotto* became so great that in
1768 the government ordered its enlargement : and the Signory was
so far from wanting to show even a superficial piety that it used funds
confiscated from convents to finance the building. By this time there
was a second *ridotto* at the S. Cassian theatre.

Families established for generations were suddenly penniless, their
palaces sold up, their farms in ruin. It got so out of hand that the
patricians had to curb themselves ; in 1774, by a vote of two hundred
and twenty 'ayes' against twenty-one 'nays' (with twenty-two ab-
stentions) the two *ridotti* were closed. The bill described the betting
there as 'solemn, continuous, universal, violent'. The buildings were
turned into government offices. Everyone grumbled, and the whole
noble class – the rich and the poor – were so bored that they started
gambling again in the cafés and their own casinos. The only thing
the government could do about that was to forbid women to go into
some of the more notorious of them, without the slightest effect.

Nothing could stop what went on in the casinos because they were private – simply houses (usually on or close by the Piazza) taken by noblemen – and quite a few noblewomen – to entertain their friends. If you closed them, which the government did at times, they simply sprouted elsewhere. The observant Beckford was taken by Mme de Rosenberg to one of them – 'a great casino which looks into the piazza, and consists of five or six rooms, fitted in a gay flimsy taste, neither rich nor elegant, where were a great many lights, and a great many ladies elegantly dressed, their hair falling very freely about them, and innumerable adventures written in their eyes. The gentlemen were lolling upon the sofas, or lounging about the apartments. The whole assembly seemed upon the verge of gaping, till coffee was carried round. This magic beverage diffused a temporary animation ; and, for a moment or two, conversation moved on with a degree of pleasing extravagance ; but the flash was soon dissipated, and nothing remained save cards and stupidity.' The stupidity, on the other hand, seemed to please Mrs Thrale, who said that all literary topics were 'pleasingly discussed at Querini's casino, where everything may be learned by the conversation of the company – but more agreeably, because women are always half the number of persons admitted here.'

Even the Church was drawn into the flimsy net of pleasure. The *abbé*, with his right both to preach and marry, wore polished shoes with bright red heels and gold or silver buckles. More often than not he was, like Casanova, fashionable to the point of foppery ; the preaching, if he did it well and was goodlooking, brought him secret loveletters, and his cloth gave him a sort of accepted sham passport to the company of ladies. A priest often lived in a noble house and was treated as little more than one of the servants ; sometimes he served refreshments to the guests, with a napkin on his shoulder. You saw few priests in company only because they were hidden in their dominos. They certainly had more liberty in Venice than elsewhere in Italy. Here the government showed a cunning appreciation of human weakness: if the priests were seen to sin like others, they lost any special mystical appeal they might have for people.

The rich in Venice had always been generous to the Church ; fortunes and lands had been bequeathed to the monasteries. Now God and money no longer went hand in hand. Church processions were more like parades. The angels in them made erotic gestures. Churches became concert halls, sparkling with sumptuous decoration. We owe the lack of goodlooking churches in Venice today to the city's wealth; Romanesque arches were torn down, 'primitive' frescoes were painted over by people impatient for gaudy decoration. The Venetians laughed and talked during Mass. Preachers were showmen. Women showed bare shoulders in church, they flirted and kissed. The confessional was a place to get rid of the dark mental effects of debauchery or gambling.

The cafés (their delicious spiced drinks pleased the women) were second homes for everybody. By the eighteenth century nearly every shop round the Piazza was one. The 'Secretaries' (high-ranking civil servants) went to the *caffé dei segretari*, the top officials to the *Nave*, the Frenchified or left-wing set to the *Spaderia*, the literary lions to the *Menegazzo*. And then, when you were tired of the casino and the opera and the *ridotto* and church and even cafés you could sit at the pharmacist's and gossip, or at the barber's or at a bookshop. Your coffee was brought to you from next door.

Yet Venice was balanced, even healthy. Six months of the year is a long time for any carnival, especially if you spend the rest of the year looking forward to it. But Venetian carnivals were never like the wild and vigorous orgies north of the Alps, in Cologne and Munich. They were never a temporary release from law and order. There was a theme of grace from beginning to end; what Carlo Gozzi called the 'lusts' of the noble class (he said they corrupted each other 'like hounds on the scent') would have looked tired in Frankfurt. The Venetian nobility was not so much jaded as over-refined. Mrs Thrale found them the happiest people in Europe. They 'scorned to contribute to the degradation of the whole by indulging a gross depravity of manners'. Even when they competed with each other in gaudy display, they showed balance by almost never bragging. The accuracy of Voltaire's portrait of Procurante, the Venetian senator in *Candide* whose palace on the Brenta is a castle of delights, lies in the fact that he never boasts about it.

Only from outside did it all look eccentric and unhinged. A Turkish sailor told his Muslim friends how these poor Christians went crazy for six months of the year but then suddenly one day they found a grey powder (the ashes strewn on the head at Lent) which cured them at once for quite forty days. How strange the domino must have looked to him, its mask like a monster-bird's beak, under the *baula* (a monster's hood) crowned by a three-cornered hat of all things – for both the men and the women. And there was so much flitting to and fro and whispering and ducking into the dark cabins of gondolas. Patricians who could afford it kept a suite of rooms in a hidden corner of town where they could escape with their girls; and not even their house-gondoliers could say where they were.

This was how William Beckford described dusk: 'I passed the gates of the palace into the great square, which received a faint gleam from its casinos and palaces, just beginning to be lighted up, and to become the resort of pleasure and dissipation. Numbers were walking in parties upon the pavement; some sought the convenient gloom of the porticos with their favourites; others were earnestly engaged in conversation, and filled the gay illuminated apartments, where they resorted to drink coffee and sorbet, with laughter and merriment. A thoughtless giddy transport prevailed; for, at this hour, anything like restraint seems perfectly out of the question; and however solemn a magistrate or senator may appear in the day, at night he lays up wig and robe and gravity to sleep together, runs intriguing about in his gondola, takes the reigning sultana under his arm, and so rambles half over the town, which grows gayer and gayer as the day declines.'

Yet the daily self-indulgence bored him: 'I wonder a lively people can endure such monotony, for I have been told the Venetians are remarkably spirited; and so eager in the pursuit of amusement as hardly to allow themselves any sleep. . . . This may be very true, and yet I will never cite the Venetians as examples of vivacity. Their nerves, unstrung by early debaucheries, allow no natural flow of lively spirits, and at best a few moments of a false and feverish activity. The approaches of sleep, forced back by an immoderate use of coffee, render them weak and listless, and the facility of being wafted from place to place in a gondola, adds not a little to their indolence. In short, I can scarcely regard their Eastern neighbours in a more hazy light ; who, thanks to their opium and their harems, pass their lives in one perpetual doze.'

Nothing summarised this Venice better than the gondola. No carriage compared with it for comfort. You could read, eat, make love in its tiny cabin, hidden from the world. It was an intoxicating gift for leisure – effortless, hushed. At sunset Venetians drifted out on the lagoon, talking, in twos and threes. The old barcarolle said, '*Vien co mi, montemo in gondola, andaremo fora in mar.*' You went 'outside' to the sea, beyond sad mortal thoughts. And what happened to Venice in the eighteenth century was like that too – a sort of sea-change : the city drifted out of its past thoughts into silence. And the sleight-of-hand of the gondoliers, sweeping their odd scooped boats through the narrow canals, brushing others with nimble skill, was very Venetian too – the smooth, secret, assured inheritance of ages.

One of the most wonderful sights was a procession of gondolas on a state occasion. The official boats were gilded and splendidly carved. The state gondoliers wore a special livery – scarlet velvet capes embroidered with gold, and huge hats.

Though the ordinary gondolas were by law black, a lot of money was still spent on the accessories, as a matter of prestige. Linings of satin and silk, mountings of ebony and inlaid ivory, liveries embroidered with gold were all at different times forbidden. But decrees were useless : they simply brought the forbidden item into vogue. Punishment for disobedience had been tough – three years in the galleys for gondoliers who made too great a show. Goethe described the gondolas as 'biers', but money was still lavished on cabin interiors. And the dark exterior helped secrecy, anonymity ; once you stepped inside you were safe from spies ; incredibly enough, no gondolier took bribes.

The loveliest of the palaces at that time were the Pesaro, the Cornaro, the Grimani, the Labia. According to President de Brosses, who saw most of them, their rooms were gorgeous without showing much taste. He noticed that the Foscarini palace had two hundred rooms extravagantly furnished but not a single comfortable chair to sit down on –

D

a very Italian state of affairs. Everything was for the eye, and you took your comfort only in the private chambers.

Everyone who went to Venice visited the Arsenal, but as a kind of theatrical experience, since its function was all but dead. The closely guarded docks contained three fountains of wine at which the workers could help themselves at any time. By the middle of the century there were about eighteen large war vessels on the stocks, surrounded by the state gondolas and the *Bucentoro*, an astonishing sight for its gilded statues supporting the vast cabin-roof, its sofas and doge's throne. Mrs Thrale saw the *Sposalizio*, in which the doge used to throw the ring of the Republic from the *Bucentoro* into the sea in a symbolic act of marriage. The *Bucentoro* she saw must have been the last of them all, built in 1728. The last time the sea was espoused was in 1796, just a few months before a mob tore every shred of gold from the *Bucentoro*'s decks, smashed the statues of Apollo and the nine muses, and of Prudence and Strength on either side of the doge's throne, and mounted four guns on the deck. The boat then became a sailor's prison.

In spite of Venice's atmosphere of easy harmlessness her reputation for easy murder still survived. Giuseppe Baretti wrote his *Manners and Customs in Italy* in answer to a surgeon of Guy's Hospital in London whose book on Italy had been full of clumsy judgements. Dr Sharp had written that Venetians would stab anybody on the smallest provocation, and that any Venetian church was a sanctuary for criminals. He then told the story of 'the late English resident' who had sworn to spare no expense should an Englishman be murdered during the term of his residentship; with the result that no Englishman had in fact been murdered. Baretti happened to have known this Resident intimately, and to have had 'a thousand conversations' with him about the cheerful nature of the common people of Venice; in fact the Resident had so endeared himself to them that they would often stop and bless him loudly in the Venetian style when he passed – 'ciera de imperador!', 'siestu benedeto!', 'caro quel muso!'. 'The Italians are no rioters,' Baretti went on, 'and hate confusion; and they are, for the greatest part, total strangers to the idea of sedition; so that they scarcely ever rise against government, not even in time of the greatest hardships. Few of the Italian nations will suffer themselves to be seized by a violent and general rage in a century, except at Naples, where the want of bread grows quite unsupportable; but in the Venetian dominions, in Tuscany, in Lombardy, in Piedmont, I never heard of the least popular insurrection, since I was born, nor think that any body can recollect any in this century.'

The Inquisitors of State still existed but their decisions had to be approved by three senators present at their meetings; these could leave the room if they threatened a harsh decree, with the result that the decree could not become law. Behind the grim stories that lingered from the past lay the most peaceful city in Europe. 'At Venice,' Baretti said, 'it is a really delightful thing to rove on a summer night about the Laguna in a gondola, and hear from several boats several bands of musicians playing and singing, the moon shining bright, the winds hushed and the water as smooth as a glass. These *serenatas*, as we call them, are seldom or never disturbed by riots, as would probably be the case in England, were such entertainments customary: and this is perhaps the only music which the Italians enjoy in silence, as if unwilling to spoil the calm and stillness of the night.'

Venice was so much a deliberately splendid product of the Venetians, such a continuous act of creation, that her artists of any time, Titian, Veronese, Tiepolo, seemed simply a part of her developing process. Even the baroque failed to spoil her: it never degenerated into the loud ebullience of the Roman schools, but kept a quality of its own. Yet Venetian baroque is extravagant to the point of madness, because mixed with the Arab and Byzantine, with even a touch of the oriental as well. The city abounded in floridly robed figures, crowded ceilings and twisted columns, in wedding-cake garlands and creamy tassles, and heavily loaded fronts like that of Sta Maria Zobenigo and S. Moisè, yet these things fell in side by side with the work of Rizzo and Bregno and the Lombardi without disturbing the serene overall picture. Venice would be much better without them, yet still they fit, with their blissful fuss about life. Even the Bridge of Sighs seemed, by the eighteenth century, predestined for its position. The Jesuits, such a power behind the baroque style in the rest of Italy – urging people to frantic expressions of zeal they did not feel – were powerless in Venice: at least that element of imposed devoutness was missing. It had always been the custom to follow Jesuits through the streets calling after them, *Andate, andate, niente pigliate, e mai ritornate !'* ('Go away, go away, take nothing with you and never come back !').

By the eighteenth century the city was as we see it now. There were few worthwhile additions to the previous epochs. The Palladian revival at the beginning of that century really revived only the bleak elements of the neo-classical, an unfeeling imitation. It was a reaction against the grandiose, like that among the painters – Longhi, Canaletto, Rosalba Carriera and the Guardi, who painted the city and its people as if there was nothing in life beyond them: no longer the pompous classical figures, no longer even a failed attempt at religion. Good taste never quite died in Venice. There was always a banker or merchant who wanted a picture ; there was a constant dealer's market for the replenishment or sale of fabulous collections. Foreigners were prepared to pay very high prices, but amazingly little art trickled out of the Republic in its last century.

The weather, which so few even of the loving travellers mention, helped ; it made a blissful foundation, with its brilliant sea-light changing to mists, its voluptuous heavy heat in the dog-days, its harsh winter wind (*che gela fin ai pensieri*) and unbearable days of *scirocco*. It was healthy, clement. The stinks of low tide were swept away by the high. When a heavy snow melted and tumbled down the roofs in the early spring thaw it could flood the streets and cellars ; in the winter of 1788 the lagoon was frozen over, and it was possible to walk the whole distance between Venice and the mainland. Pavilions were set up and bonfires lit. From time to time there were floods in Venice as there are today, and at high tide the gondolas could sometimes navigate the big *campi* and the Piazza itself ; people were carried through the streets by porters, the women took their shoes off and paddled. The city could squeeze joy out of anything. The climax of pleasure-seeking in the eighteenth century was only a long tradition set free.

And the sea was always there, lapping against the *fondamenta* and the stout wooden piles. The sewage and kitchen slops all went into it, tugged away down the canals. The sea was a reminder of infinity, always at the edge of daily life. Its moods were in the people too, in the government they had formed, going from brightness, from brilliant pageantry, to the dark, secret, misty, implacable.

....

Chapter 5

The Artists and Venetian Light

The Ca' Rezzonico on the Grand Canal is Venice's memorial to the eighteenth century. The costumes on show are few, the furniture is set round the walls with no imagination, the place is cruelly unheated in winter, a shell into which a museum has been emptied, but it does give us an idea of the light rosy atmosphere, faint and frail and frivolous, in which the patricians lived. The building was started in 1660 by Longhena on a commission by the San Barnaba branch of the Buon (or Bon) family. Due to lack of money the work petered out over the next twenty years, so that when Longhena died only the ground and first floor were finished. For over fifty years it stayed like that, under an improvised wooden roof, as we can see from one of Canaletto's pictures: and the Buon family lived at the back. Then in 1746 they sold up to the Rezzonici, a Lombard family who had settled in Venice in the early part of the sixteenth century and made a fortune. In six years the roof was on and in another four the Grand Canal façade was finished, following Longhena's intentions but not without losing his gravity, which we still see in the dark, swelling pillars of the ground floor, in the old men's heads that stare down into the windows, the lions' faces underneath the sills, and the slim, curved steps leading down to the water. The top floor looks as if it had been forced on (though where the proportions are different is difficult to see). It belongs to just another epoch – free, airy, spacious – while the earlier floors below, with their deep-set windows, intimate and dark, their solid, thick-pillared frames carved with precisely the same motif of heads and putti, are self-assured and stolidly immobile, suggesting not a quest for freedom but self-attainment to the point of satiety, the kind of wealthy repose we see today in the Ca' Pesaro – also Longhena's work.

It was ready in time for the crowning of Pope Clement XIII (Carlo Rezzonico) which took place inside the palace in 1758. The façade was probably finished by Massari, though Gian Antonio Gaspari had a hand in the first designs. And Massari rebuilt the back of the house, giving it its present grand, turning staircase and the vast ballroom that crosses the palazzo sideways, parallel to the Grand Canal, taking up two floors with its height. In the eighteenth century styles were played with. There was no decided approach; fashions followed each other too fast. There was only one consistent theme, one demand throughout – that the mind should find repose, be softened or flattered out of thought. And if any one thing drove Venice's finest artists away, it was this. Goldoni, Tiepolo, Vivaldi, Rosalba Carriera – they all died far away.

What we see inside the palace today has little to do with its appearance at the time, apart from Tiepolo's ceilings and the fixtures. Even the floor has been replaced with ugly crushed marble. The palace changed hands several times in the nineteenth century until Robert Browning bought it as his last home: his study is one of the loveliest rooms in the building, facing the Grand Canal, its side-window looking down on the narrow Rio di San Barnaba. In 1935 it was bought by the town, and the eighteenth-century exhibits of the Museo Correr were tipped into it, to suffer the same damp in unheated rooms as they had suffered in their former home.

The ballroom is over-painted and really gives no great sense of luxury: but arrogant display was not an ideal at this time, as you can see if you look at the porcelain exhibits on the attic floor, at the chandeliers and delicate damask-covered walls, at the *chinoiserie* in the form of swelling lacquered chests and flourishing console-tables and imitation vases. Display as an end in itself was too vulgar for Venice by this late date. The tallness of the ballroom is more than an eye-catching feat: it is another effort to fly away, to become unsubstantial, to put a mask on the detail of life. It actually redeems the vast size, stops it from being a bare, cold hall. The slim windows, taking up much of three walls, do the same service, flooding it with distilled, water-reflecting light. They thus prevent the ceiling painting (by Gian Battista Crosato) from being oppressive. The two chandeliers are original, made of wood and gilded copper, graceful and delicately elaborate, their stems curling up into little rosettes, their candle-bases in the form of little crowns.

The rooms the Venetians liked best were the private ones, where no effort was made at *figura* and even the chairs were comfortable, and where above all it was warm in winter. Upstairs on the second floor a bedroom has been transplanted from a country villa with its *retrès* or side-closets, all mounted on a wooden platform like a little house on its own. One of the *retrès* is a dressing room and the other a tiny corridor leading into a delightful back parlour, secret and small, where the walls have subtle rococo designs of long twining stems and flowers; its only door is that leading into the bedroom, which itself is hardly more than a great bed framed round with wood and sliding doors, its front closed by a curtain. The bed-head of carved wood is an extravagantly florid design in tempera, with putti and a central *Madonna and Child*; the wallpaper in the rest of the room is in the black-and-white *chiaroscuro* style fashionable at that time, a print of ruins repeated over and over.

Everywhere in the palace there is lacquered, bulging, delicate furniture, with its sense of a last order touched with grace. In the so-called Calbo-Crotta room (this is the name of the country villa from which so many of the exhibits came) there is 'Chinese' work in deep-green and gold, a motif repeated in chairs and softly *bombé* sideboards and console-tables, melting in with the cloth on the wall, with the pelmets over the doors and windows, with the wall-panel beadings and the tall framed mirrors. Each room has its separate motif, rose or green or yellow, always touched with gold, enhanced behind curtains that filter the strong Venetian light. The taste for Chinese styles – in vases, chests of drawers, lacquered doors, in fans and porcelain figures, tapestries and imaginary landscapes – was one of the French fashions that caught like a fire, not that anyone knew or cared about the real China. Its remoteness was its attraction.

A rich family of that time required every article in its houses to show taste and care, even the small terra-cotta stoves which served as charcoal braziers ; hardly a surface was left undecorated. But there must be nothing that oppresses, even with luxury ; the eye should be able to glance and turn away lightly, with only the gentlest impression left behind. In all those little pictures of daily life by Pietro Longhi we see the same thing suggested – soft, fleeting conversations over chocolate, whispered remarks, long, leisured dressing while *cicisbei* and dressmaids stand by. There is so much grace, in fact, so much deliberate lightness, that something must be wrong. If you change fashions as quickly as the Venetians did, in music and clothes and painting and plays, you must be avoiding certain subjects very hard. 'What of soul was left, I wonder, when the kissing had to stop ?' Robert Browning asked in his poem on a toccata of Galuppi's. But then that was the danger of Venetian life, that you let the tides look after your conscience, taking it down the canals to the sea every day, as if the city and not you were in charge. That was what brought Thomas Mann's hero down, in the decayed aftermath of this eighteenth-century world, in a last fling of mad hope brought on by Venice's apparent position at the edge of heaven – or hell, according to how you felt. This Venice strains at the senses, lures and flatters and burns, in a sea-light that changes every hour and presents a new, unexpectedly subtle picture, so that her painters say that realism is impossible with a Venetian subject for the simple reason that before you have got half-way the mask has changed.

Of course the conversations in those little bedrooms and the closets of retreat were not really soft : apart from the fact that Venetians have the loudest voices even in Italy, they have always been a practical people ; they produced no poetry to speak of. Wherever patrician women and *cicisbei* meet in Goldoni's plays there is shouting and quarrelling, though of the brotherly kind. The point about the conversation was its sweet tone, thrilling with intimacy, sung, whatever arguments were going on. Once we have heard the real dialect (rare today outside the markets of the Canareggio district, and on the islands) we know that the softness was not a matter of sound at all but feeling. No dialect in Italy – or rather, no way of speaking Italian, since Venetian is not strictly a dialect – bears such a sense of the other person in its tones, such a minute, witty expressiveness, with its words like *stomeghezzi*, meaning 'unbearable little things', *pampalughetto* for 'a little ass', its *siora* and *cara ela* addressed by one woman to another, its softening of *madre* into *mare*, *figlio* into *fio*, *il padrone* into *el paròn*, *sior* for *signore*, and the gentle, almost Spanish hiss of words like *cossa* for *cosa*, *cussì* for *così*, *lassare* for *lasciare*, and *zorno* for *giorno*, *dasseno* for *davvero*, the turning of *dico* into *digo*, *sicuro* into *siguro*, making it rushed, clipped, sweetly secretive, so that quite un-Italian sounding sentences like *Se nol ghe n'ha el ghe ne pol aver* ('if he hasn't got them, he can always get them') become possible.

In all the dialect plays of Goldoni there is no more Venetian scene than that in *Todero Brontolon* between Marcolina and Fortunata, where in a few very pointed sentences softened by endearments they strike a marriage-bargain involving Marcolina's daughter. The youth is called *el putto* ('child'), and the girl *la putta*. '*El putto xè una pua, xè una pasta de marzapan !*', Fortunata tells her – 'the child is a gem, a marzipan paste!'. When the bargain is sealed, Fortunata asks if the boy may see the girl, and when she gets the gently unyielding, '*Co sarà serà el contratto*' ('When the contract is signed'), cries, '*Eh ! via, cara ela, che al dì d'ancuo le se vede le putte. No se sta più su sti rigori, no : le se vede*' – 'Away with you, my dear, nowadays the children see each other. These old rules don't apply any more ; they see each other!'. To translate the dialect-plays into Italian, let alone a third language, takes away half of their sweet, biting power.

Such a language could never have been used languorously. The picture of a languorous patrician class in Venice at any time is a wrong one. They had plenty to talk about, mostly trifles, but these excited and stirred. The Venetian theatres were a riot of tomfoolery before the curtain went up ; the walls shook with noise. The long silences that Beckford noticed at the *casino*, which only coffee could break into speech, were much more due to the Italian nature than to languor of feeling. Italian silences have always been signs of contentment, not of empty-mindedness. Mrs Thrale was nearer the mark here when she said, 'Whoever seeks to convince instead of persuade an Italian, will find he has been employed in a Sisyphean labour ; the stone may roll to the top, but is sure to return and rest at his feet who had the courage to try the experiment. Logic is a science they love not, and, I think, steadily refuse to cultivate ; nor is argument a style of conversation they naturally affect.'

And Venice was created by logic as little as it excited logic in its admirers ; if anything it made them impatient with everything they had known before ; they began to think it absurd to build cities on land. We must never forget the illogical sea that was always present under the window, at the side of the *calle*, shining in the distance, separating the islands, rising and falling in a rhythm that made little of men and logic ; and the reviving air that seeped through the closed windows, quickly mending the effect of a dissipated night. While this strange city invited dissipation it also stirred health, which is why the historians can never decide whether she was really debauched in the eighteenth century or a happy, well-functioning little state to her last day. What would be a debauched life in a land-city is a different affair in Venice.

But perhaps the most contradictory thing about the city, a sign of the strangeness of its powers, is the fact that it has made its artists its own like no other in the peninsula ; yet it never paid more than a grudging attention to artistic values. In an odd way all Venetian art from that of the Bellinis to Tiepolo's son is state art. Yet the state is like no other ; it is never quite the hard, mortal world usually conveyed by that word. The painters and architects, the *quadraturiste* who painted mock-pillars and balconies and cornices for angels and putti to tumble over, the furniture-makers and porcelain-glazers and silk-weavers, the stucco-artists, the glass-blowers and dress-makers, the craftsmen of chandeliers, of marionnettes and ornate gilded mirror-frames, of gaily painted toilet-chests, were all passionately willing servants of the Serenissima, which was never quite the actual government, never quite the Ten, if only because the Ten changed every six months and what was last year's rejection might be this year's commission. Anyone who has left Venice with a drowsy, resentful feeling that, being not quite in the world, she should not be leavable like other places, knows why men fought and schemed to get back to her

though they knew it meant their death, why even foreigners gave
themselves up to her guiles.

The whole course of Venetian art can be seen as a blissful attempt to
define Venetian light, until with Tiepolo in the eighteenth century
there is only the light left. There is no subject any longer, not even
much of a feeling: just the fullness of the light, glittering, searching,
flooding everything ; and when he leaves for Spain, and settles down
there, the figures and powerful composition remain but the light has
gone.

Painter after painter gloried in the act of painting as an end in itself.
Tintoretto simply could not find enough walls to work on ; pictures
poured out of him ; if he had been condemned to paint apples all his
life he would have done it, and perhaps said as much. That was Venice's
beguiling, dangerous side. Again and again, when we pass vast walls
like those in the Council chamber of the ducal palace, celebrating
a victory or a legend from Venice's past or a forgotten coronation,
we may wonder if the artists ever stopped to ask themselves, 'Why
am I painting?'. The answer might have been that they were too happy
to stop. It is what makes Venetian art the most steadily profane of
any in the peninsula.

Until the eighteenth century, when Piazzetta started the College of
Painters, which became the present *Accademia*, painters were members of a guild like any other artisan ; they were in the strictest sense
servants, and they never, unless like Titian they reached the noble
class, thought themselves otherwise. They subscribed to a *mariegola*
or charter ; and this is true of the Bellinis and Giorgione in the late
fifteenth century, of Carpaccio, of Titian and Tintoretto at the beginning of the sixteenth century, and of Paolo Veronese a little later.
They were on the same social level as house-painters: and as house-
painters – or church-painters – they began. They had to pass through
an apprenticeship in the *bottegha* of a master. Unless they were inscribed on the guild-register they were unable to sell their work, and
if they did sell outside their workshops they were fined ten lire. At
no time in Titian's life, even when he had one of the grandest houses

in the lagoon (according to a popular story the Emperor Charles V was happy to pick up a fallen brush for him), did he cease to observe guild rules.

Painting was definitely a lay act, and Venice made it so. The examination of Paolo Veronese by the Holy Office in 1573 to investigate his motives in painting as part of a *Last Supper* a jester with a parrot, St Peter carving a roast, drunken Germans, a dwarf and a servant with a nose-bleed was a casual affair precisely because the man under accusation was a painter, that is, a man of the people. His excuse for the figures was that the canvas was a very big one (about seventeen by forty feet) and he had to fill it somehow. Also, as he had been told that the Last Supper took place in a rich man's house, he thought he had a chance to show great magnificence and spread it all over the seventeen by forty feet. A minor excuse was that Michelangelo had also shown little religious sense when he painted everyone in his *Last Judgement* in the nude (which must be about the most philistine thing ever said by a major painter). The inquisitors, in fact, showed more taste and delicacy than he did ; they gave him a mild order to scrub the wrong figures out, which he disregarded by changing the title.

Really his *Supper in the House of Levi*, as it became, is a brawl, with Christ as chairman. It is an extraordinary document of the collapse of religion in sixteenth-century Venice, at a time of what is usually regarded as a Catholic revival. In his work we have the self-assurance of a powerful state whose habits are so complete, so mysteriously sacred, that they leave no time for the solitary artistic act. Veroneses are superbly executed, in the grandest Venetian style, as if nothing existed beyond the human and social, and state authority had replaced the human.

It was the climax of the religious nullity (not at all scepticism) that had been eating its way into art, and therefore into life, since Giovanni Bellini first transmuted the set sacred subjects inherited from the Byzantine world into the fields and hills and woods actually seen by the eye. His madonnas become honest Friulian girls, gazing down at the holy child with a strong native pride. In Giovanni Bellini and

Carpaccio too you have a hint of what will later become baroque posturing, a touch of the later insincerity. There is marvellous atmosphere – always the strength of the Venetian schools. But perhaps these painters would willingly have lived in other epochs when holy subjects could have been given up : not through any impatience with holy subjects, but through a protestant conviction that holiness is conveyed most through secular life. The relaxed ease in Giorgione derives from his use of secular life as a subject, without conventional signs. In his works, or what we suppose to be his works, a warm light diffuses the landscape ; life is grasped at one of its points of bliss. And bliss was conveyed by the Venetian painter in light.

As in Perugino, everything in a Giorgione landscape seems to float in light ; in the strange *Tempest* the round, placid figure of the woman suckling her child, and the nearby man leaning casually on his staff, while a storm breaks behind them, are held together in a moment of hushed unity, as if space and time were thrown over suddenly, and the still core of life touched. That was religious experience brought into secular terms, because the old Byzantine images no longer had more than an institutional appeal, however fruitful their influence on Umbrian and Sienese schools.

And then with Tintoretto and Titian there is this wonderful rehabilitation of nature, imbued through and through with divinity, taken a step further until it becomes a conscious celebration ; something too spectacular even for warm feelings has been achieved. With the superb, dazzling performance, so unhesitating and assured, we see the beginning of self-indulgence, where the object seen is so explored for its divinity that nothing is left over to kindle feeling. This is not completely true of either artist, least of all Titian. But if that is the way we want to look at their work – as a dazzling performance – we can : for the first time we have painting that can be admired by senators and *Savi* and busy merchants ; we have the beginning of a sparkling commodity that appeals to men who want their art stated without problems, where you can say that not a line or a colour is wrong. In Tintoretto the professional flair is at the expense of almost everything else. His *Madonna dei Tesioreri* is in a smooth, natural style,

but with no end beyond itself: it is just a picture. In his *Assumption*
the effect is simply of an animated crowd. He can do anything with
a brush. The background of his *Removal of St Mark's Body* is so
hurried as to be a sketch. But he can get away with it.

And a portrait by Titian was the last word about the sitter. We feel
we need never look beyond his portraits of Philip of Spain and
Alfonso d'Avalos, or the unbelievable double portrait of the Emperor
Charles v and Isabella, for a verification of their personalities. But he is
nearly incapable of a sacred subject. In his classical subjects there is
a sense of flesh so rich that they are almost sensuous and nothing else.
In the sacred subjects there is no advance beyond this: the sensuous
heaviness shows through as absence of spirit – not spirit as a baroque
posture (there is a strong hint of that), but spirit like the diffused light
in Giorgione. His *Noli me tangere* is only just this side of the erotic,
as though that was the point of Christ's unwillingness to be touched.
His *Madonna suckling the Child* (in the National Gallery, London) is
almost a patrician woman, with no sacred reference at all. His *Doge
Grimani kneeling before Faith*, his *Descent of the Holy Spirit*, above
all his *Christ appearing to the Virgin Mary* have the kind of sentimentality that the worst baroque artists charged their sacred subjects
with for the good reason that they had no strong feelings to convey.
His *Christ bearing the Cross* at S. Rocco captures the Passion as an
experience, like a moment snatched from a busy life full of brilliant
talk. In Titian we see how the classical subject began historically as
a liberation for the artist from medieval thinking, and gradually became a vehicle of self-satisfaction, until the first sense of spirituality
was lost; and 'spirit' became the bleak mental detachment which is
mostly what we mean by the word today.

Titian is capable of the spirit, but it is thrown in at the end, so
to speak. In his *Baptist* (at the Accademia) it is conveyed in one tiny
point, the gleaming white of the Baptist's eye, which redeems the
whole picture. His work can be taken two ways: you can keep it
on the surface, as the perfect realisation of atmosphere, or you can
read the suffering. His *Pietà* (also in the Accademia) has this duality.
It was the most officially acceptable art ever done by a great man.

But the officials were Venetian: this was what made such a duality possible. Venetian officialdom was like no other in Christendom. It made the only acceptable state-art we know.

Right at the beginning of Venetian art, in the lay scenes of Gentile Bellini and Carpaccio, you have a fascination with light which becomes obsessive in the later painters. Gentile's *Procession in St Mark's Square* (in the Accademia) with its hundreds of figures and the glowing rose-brown of the square itself (paved with crossed bricks until the middle of the eighteenth century), with the clustered golden steeples of the Basilica and the bronze horses backed by dark domes, creates a mellow light to which the sky, when we glance at it, comes as a surprise. And there is the same effect of surprising contrast, full of brooding atmosphere, in Carpaccio's *The Miracle of the Relic of the True Cross*.

Atmosphere is everything. The Carpaccio room in the Accademia is heavy with it. In Veronese light becomes resolved into colour: there is no colourist like him in all Venetian art, just as for composition Tintoretto has no superior. In Veronese the light seems to come from the sea, penetrating corners with its sparkle, and exploited to the full as an element of luxury, like the brocades and jewels and laces on his women. Sixteenth-century Venice teemed with physical power. Yet in his *Annunciation* Veronese achieved something almost religious, certainly quite beyond opulence alone: the picture has a stillness untypical of him, though it is spoilt by the Virgin's cheap look of expectation. In subjects where intimacy counted (so powerfully intimate was Venetian life) he says something beyond the paint, as in the *Coronation of the Virgin*. But where family intimacy counts for nothing, as in *The Crucifixion*, we have another of his lavish brawls.

It all adds up to this: that Venetian life exercised a continual and overwhelming influence on the artist, stirring the magicians like Tintoretto and Veronese to an unceasing bacchanalia of work, and tempting great powers like those of Titian to fall into the sensuous. Under her influence painting became a quest for *bliss*, and too often the bliss was found in the act of painting itself.

If the eighteenth century could be summarised in a picture perhaps it would be Gian Battista Piazzetta's charcoal drawing of *A Nude Woman in the Sun* (1735–40). After centuries of symbolism, allegory and posturing, and the showy mechanics of light and shade – all the paraphernalia which entranced painters in the sixteenth century and became a ruinous decadence in the seventeenth – we suddenly have something like the modern world. The nude woman runs one of her hands down her leg, in a slow, wondering movement ; you can almost feel the sun on her back, salty from the sea, warming her through. Nothing could be less pretentious. She is neither a patrician nor a lace-worker nor a fisherwoman nor a Friulian nor a Secretary's wife, but a woman.

It shows that the *ancien régime* was only a masque kept going for a century, not the real life of Venice (Ippolito Nievo described the Serenissima in her last years as 'a tomb of noblemen in which a healthy people was locked up'), any more than foppishness was the life of England or France in the same period. Venice's *ancien régime* was the froth on top: everything in the drawing-rooms, in the *ridotti* and *casini*, in the ballrooms and the bedrooms, even in the gondolas at night when the *felze*-curtains were closed, amounted to froth. At the opera and the playhouse there was froth or humour ; when the Venetians had laughed their fill at Goldoni (recognising in his work their superbly unified society) they turned to the fables of Carlo Gozzi, without the slightest attention to the question of which of the two could really write, above all which of them spoke the truth. The truth, as far as this delightful, nervous, hollow masque was concerned, had nothing pleasant about it.

Yet the truth could only be laughed at so good-naturedly (and good nature is the key to eighteenth-century Venice) if there was repose underneath. And the repose is what marks out Venice from every other place in Europe. You see it in Piazzetta's charcoal drawing, shorn of class, pride, luxury. And in another of his pieces, more famous than the charcoal drawing – *The Fortune Teller*, done in 1740. Here the old Venetian concern with light comes out: it is almost a Caravaggio. The Venetians, after all, had no mountains or wooded landscapes to en-close shade in endless varieties of colour ; what they saw were buildings

E

and the sea, mitigated here and there by a garden ; it was the light from the sea and sky that changed, and buildings were merely surfaces for the display of this light, from the brooding stillness of mist to the brilliance of *tramontana*. You have Venetian light clear and strong in Carpaccio, rosy and fine as dust in Giorgione, dramatic and contrasted in the Veneziani, in Bellini and Titian, above all in the man who believed that the two best colours were black and white, and who was accused by the critic Longhi of simply messing about like a stage director with 'machines' for rain, lightning and other dramatic outbursts of nature – Tintoretto. In this *Fortune Teller* of Piazzetta's the light is displayed effortlessly, as if the whole problem had at last been resolved, in fact as if there were no problem any longer, only a state of ease bordering on laughter.

If we compare the painted porcelain vases and the bronze ornaments of the sixteenth century with those of the later centuries we shall find that the first have a serious, downright opulence, while the latter are gaudy. In fact gaudiness tended to be the Venetian taste in all ages, but never before had it lacked solemn assurance ; it had never been cloying. In the seventeenth century, however, taste begins to wobble. Domenico Rizzi designed the inside of the *Gesuiti* with a mass of gilded stucco and vividly coloured marble, aiming at the strange and striking, no longer at a comfortable assertion of wealth. The balance of the first baroque has gone. Anything is done to twist a line, make flourishes, scrolls, ribbons, bows ; figures hang from the ceiling, protrude from elaborate corniced walls ; there are marble drapes. Every salon is a wedding-cake of ivory-inlaid tables and chair-covers of satin and velvet, with mirrors, statues, busts, putti, all contrasting with the austere lines of the palace outside, which usually belonged to an earlier Venice.

The imagination has become fervently energetic : yet without real power ; it is *only* inventive, *only* original – the signs of an imagination not engaged with great themes. The actual power of Venice lay in her dark and melancholy foyers, belonging to *palazzi* built before the age of extravagance. But they depressed the modern Venetian : the moment you entered his private apartments an outburst of colour and light met you. A ceiling was often so dressed in plaster as to look like a canopy: in the *Salone dei Putti* of the Palazzo Albrizzi, decorated at the end of the seventeenth century, a great central frame billows out in stucco pleats, supported at the edges by more than life-size figures, while putti float among the pleats themselves. When ceilings were not teeming with stucco flowers and coats of arms, trumpeting angels and festoons and flowing ribbons, they were painted, and had massive glittering chandeliers underneath them. Not a spot of wall or ceiling could be left alone, as if decay and emptiness might otherwise show through. Some fear was clearly being exorcised. Colours too changed. They were paler and finer and mistier now: the Rosalba Carriera miniatures, painted with the drawing room in mind, repeat these lovely colours again and again, as if the only light that fell on Venice was distilled by curtains, broken by vividly painted walls, not made by clouds and mists any more. The materials used are lighter ; the designs are smaller ; everything is put under a veil ; the heavy chairs and tables of the seventeenth century are gone ; it is all rose, gilt, gentle green now, in designs of sinuous stems and slim birds, always cheerful and light, to please but never to ravish.

Chapter 6

The Last Great Artists
of the Republic

Gianbattista Tiepolo, born a hundred and fifty years after Veronese, resolved that artist's sense of colour into terms of light. Brocades and velvets and superb lacework were no longer needed. Light shines up into faces, bleaching and lining them. It defines hands like a microscope, makes every blue a sea-blue, every white blinding. Everything seems blown by a fine, sandy wind from the Adriatic, in an eternal beach-world where there is no need to study shade and cloud because these are only diminutions of light. Therefore the sky is his subject again and again. His freedom is there. He has no subjects, only different places pierced with light. Where warm light poured itself mildly over a Giorgione landscape, it is now studied in its reflections, as if the landscape counted only in its function of showing light. In the long *Il Serpente di Bronzo* at the Accademia it is difficult to realise that suffering is involved, that the mother on the right, her breast protruding towards her child as if still fertile, is dead – only the gleaming grey of her skin tells us so, as an afterthought. The work is really beyond feeling, concern ; there is nothing to suggest that religion ever existed or was necessary ; and yet the fulcrum of religion – the sense that there exists a certain kind of bliss beyond pleasure and pain – is there. The sky breaks open ; cornices split (but only so that they may sparkle in the sun) ; figures float as never before in painting. They are suspended in space by nature, congenitally ; they lose their decaying, mortal elements. It is a marvellous stage presentation, a last attempt in the old tradition to paint the sacred.

By the eighteenth century the real world is so cloying, suffocating, anguishing that Tiepolo can find nothing in it he wants to paint. Modern society has come into being ; people begin to occupy more and more of each other's thoughts ; these block out their light, impede their

development. Tiepolo has to make his people float, take away the
heaviness of their flesh. But the subjects he chooses have no meaning.
They simply record his quest for freedom.

That flight and floating were a painter's mania at the time (partly
created by so many ceilings to fill) is obvious. The ceiling and walls
of the ballroom in the Palazzo Rezzonico, *The Allegory of the Four
Parts of the World*, done by Gian Battista Crosato in 1755, with their
putti, pillars, cornices, statues sitting perilously on the edge of niches,
mock-balconies bursting from the walls, horses and robed figures gleaming in the sunlight, are like Tiepolo, but without his redeeming power
of joy. *The Nuptials of Ludovico Rezzonico with Faustina Savorgnan*
(1758) in the second salon is by Tiepolo. The couple is mounted
on Apollo's chariot, drawn by two white horses that plunge across
the clouds, while an old man (his boot in the image of another old
man's face) holds up a flag with their two coats of arms on it ; a
blinded cupid floats under the carriage and clouds spray over the sides
of the painted balcony. Three putti float holding a mirror for the bride ;
there is a floating trumpeter. Another of his ceilings in the same palace,
Strength and Wisdom (1744–5), gives an unbelievable sense of im-
mensity ; birds wheel in the far distance of the light-blue sky, the sun
shines on the billowy folds of Strength's gown ; the breasts of the
two women are light, full, milky, delicate. You only have to compare Lazarini's work of the same period to see how grounded the
baroque style was by this time, what flights Tiepolo had to take to
escape its heavy, posturing, over-fleshy limbs. And Gaspare Diziani's
ceiling, *Poetry Triumphing over all the Other Arts*, shows just how
earthbound floating figures can be.

The Triumph of Zephyr and Flora, Tiepolo's other ceiling, has a
delicately sensuous appeal ; the naked man and woman glow in the sunrise as he holds her round the waist with light fingers ; their flesh is
as soft as velvet. His *Allegory of Merit* (some ridiculous question as to
whether 'Nobility' or 'Integrity' is higher), which he painted for the
Rezzonico bedchamber (1758), shows Merit as an old man crowned with
bay leaves going up to the temple of glory, with Nobility by him as a
winged angel. Another angel-trumpeter and an area of sky have

suffered from the damp, having been removed from the Barbarigo palace at Sta Maria del Griglio, for which it was originally painted; so there is little impression of space in this one. His *Strength and Wisdom* was painted on canvas and then attached to the ceiling, so that we have it in its first brilliance: he certainly never did a finer piece, where warmth and coolness are conveyed simultaneously in a still sky. These were his last works before he left for Spain, invited there as court-painter, at the age of sixty-two.

The titles of Tiepolo's pieces could all be forgotten, and mostly we do forget them. Only the blissful light evokes feeling; otherwise we look at his work in a state as detached as one of his figures, and perhaps we were intended to. Sometimes, as in the putto who floats upside down in his *Allegory of Merit*, the virtuosity strikes us.

In a way it is what Tintoretto's vitality (in the present fraudulent sense of that word) had been leading to: Tintoretto's love of movement and speed and surprise, the great wind that carries everything along with it, never pausing to take stock, is stilled in Tiepolo. A pause is reached, the last one there is; since there is no space and time in his works, there can only be stillness; since there is really no flesh there are no names, therefore no themes; calling the figures Virtues was just a way of differentiating one piece from another; his mature work is really one painting.

The mellow ease of Venetian life, which lies behind the work of the best artists, is conveyed to us most directly in portraits. Tintoretto's portrait of Battista Morosini, a busy matter-of-fact face weathered by many seas, conveys mellow self-assurance to perfection: Morosini stands relaxed, but as if on his way somewhere, just pausing for a moment, his thoughts elsewhere. His *Doge Alvise Mocenigo* has the same immediate quality. The skin is always in bloom. And that sense of bloom in the human face – autumnal and not far from being rotten now – is expressed in a last, adoring glance in the eighteenth century by Rosalba Carriera. She shows us the patricians in their repose; the weather-beaten, practical, assured look of the earlier face has gone. Every line, in face and dress, is light, soft, gracious. The lace gleams bright, the hair is like down, hands and shoulders are easy, un-concerned ; lips are set placidly, smiling, as if bliss is a daily experience. And to show us that she did not dream these faces into being, but drew what she saw, we have one of the softest and most sweetly reposeful portraits done by another artist, one of Tiepolo's sons, Lorenzo, in a style undistinguishable from Rosalba's – *Woman with a Fan*; she holds a closed fan lightly between two fingers, a slight smile on her lips, her eyes reflective, tolerant, penetrating. It is the face of Francesco Guardi's mother.

The moment Rosalba goes outside the patrician class, to convey piety, her touch is gone. The *Nun Praying* is pallid, hard-lined, unsmiling, as if the idea of withdrawing from life (from Venetian life too !) had failed to work out. The praying hands are false, over-drawn. But Rosalba's other faces, whether of children, women young and old, men in armour or men in easy clothes, are rounded with health, ripe and unstinted, clear-eyed, their complexions cleansed and coloured by sea-air. How-ever much they locked themselves to a card-table, that air got to all of them. Perhaps her loveliest piece is the portrait of an unnamed *Gentleman* (Room XVII in the Accademia) for its light-blue, fading delicacy, the face plump but with nothing weathered about it ; there is the slight smile again, the eyes are distant, soft, as if the only discipline they had ever exercised or suffered was that of untiring politeness.

Rosalba is recognised at once by her filmy pastel shades, the delicate rose, the light blue and creamy white ; by the sweet cast of features (absent only in her self-portraits). The child holding the *ciambella* (a breakfast roll shaped like a ring and as big as a hand) looks as if angels had reared him. Only the foreigners (Cardinal Melchior de Polignac, *Abbé* Leblond) have something in the set of the mouth that is not quite ravished with delight, and therefore seem not to be Venetian of the period.

It is odd to compare Tiepolo, the author of grand ceilings, with Rosalba Carriera, miniaturist and portraitist of the patrician class. But their work has this in common, that it states no problem : the sun-lit figures ; their world is finished, closed to further development. yielding, soft expressions of the portraits are the same as the floating,

The moment these artists, at opposite ends of development, attempt a real subject the effect is lost. Of all Venice's eighteenth-century artists, perhaps only Piazzetta and Francesco Guardi tried to convey meaning.

The worst in Piazzetta, like his *Alexander and Darius*, is like a stage-set, with obvious lighting. But his *Crucifixion*, a small canvas in the Accademia, rejects all effects. It is dark. The place is deserted; it must be at night, in the two or three hours when we sleep deepest. Blood pours from Christ's feet. A wind ruffles the scrap of cloth at his loins. The crown of thorns is clear in the darkness; only a bright light falling on one side of the body makes it visible at all. This is a remarkable canvas for eighteenth-century Venice. The sincerity is a surprise: so is such a direct statement. Even in his *Fortune Teller* there is sincerity – 'even' because it is in the accepted contemporary style. There is something of Carpaccio's seriousness, a certain measured way of putting on paint. Piazzetta's self-portrait in the Ca' Rezzonico shows him observant, serious, concentrated.

The work of both Tiepolo and Piazzetta (not to mention the realistic Canaletto) was a reaction against the highly decorative baroque of the first ten years of the century, or what some people call the rococo. This reaction really began with Federico Bencovitch, a Dalmatian born in Venice in 1677. Light and atmosphere begin to dominate frenzied decorative composition. The tone is suddenly serious, immobile: the violent and dramatic are thrown away as a tiresome mannerism, a false vitality. In Bencovitch there is a hint of Piazzetta in the way he uses light, and of Tiepolo in a certain fragile weightlessness in his figures, for instance in *The Sacrifice of Iphigenia* and his *Hagar and Ishmael in the Desert*, both of them in Marburg. He and Piazzetta took lessons from the same master, Giuseppe Maria Crespi, in Milan.

Piazzetta's interest in the light-contrasts of Caravaggio gave his themes something dramatic, but it was no longer the baroque mock-drama, that is rhetoric. In his conventional pictures, like *St James led to his Martyrdom* in the church of S. Stae, and *The Sacrifice of Isaac* in the Owen Fenwick Collection in London, the distinction from the old baroque is difficult to establish: the staged posture is still there, but

....

The stones of Venice
OPPOSITE The doge's palace
OVERLEAF Piazza San Marco

this time it is all done with sincerity. His portrait of Giulia Lama, also in London, has a modern quality, a tenderness and sense of delicate reminiscence, without any of the foppish delicacy of his time, which for a moment puts him nearer to the English painters than to other Venetians. There is even a possibility in his work of a return to religious gravity, a sudden harking back to Giovanni Bellini, to the Veneziani; but it never exceeds a possibility. You see it in *The Madonna and the Guardian Angel*, with its figures in tiers, a great light shining across them towards the angel (in the museum at Kassel). And his *Assumption of the Virgin Mary* in the Louvre would be the same baroque romp towards the sky as in thousands of pictures everywhere on the Italian mainland were it not for the fact that he actually seems to feel the subject: the Virgin really does seem to rise with a terrific light force, while the group below is static, bound, mortal. His ceiling at the church of Ss. Giovanni e Paolo in Venice is an extraordinary affair of floating figures in a blinding sky, like Tiepolo taken to a point of drama where almost a message – and this is saying a lot for the eighteenth century – comes through ; but again it has an 'as-if' quality ; it remains a *painting* of a religious experience and not the experience itself. Perhaps in the end his best work lay in his portraits (the tender *Portrait of the Young Sculptor*, for instance) and his charcoal and chalk drawings (*A Nude Woman in the Sun* and his delightful *El Boccolo*, 'the rosebud'), where the touch is light and suggestive, the sincerity unstrained. Perhaps his nearest to a religious picture (the demands of a corrupted Church have to be remembered) was his *Ecstasy of St Francis*, in the museum at Vicenza. St Francis seems to lie in exhaustion, held afloat by an angel, dreaming, his eyes closed but not really asleep. Yet the lay pictures convey more of the substance of religious feeling, even when they are apparently sensuous, like *The Pastorale* (in the Chicago museum), where the sitting woman has bare feet, and shows one breast, and the tiny boy is naked below his waist.

Next to Tiepolo and the tender and dramatic Piazzetta, the work of Francesco Guardi looks fragmentary, rushed, as if only a moment was available in which to record the light ; but in this quick glance he captures more of the atmosphere of Venice than any other artist

....
Church of the Salute

of the time. Naturally enough, it was only after the Impressionists
that his reputation become solid. *The Bucentaur at S. Niccolò di Lido*
(in the Louvre) with its fine blues for the shaded water against the
dashes of orange and red for the flags and the oars, and the touch of
gold from an ambassadorial gondola in the distance, all briefly stated,
is worlds away from the hot, blinding, drowsily crowded *La Festa della
Sensa* (Ascension Day Celebration), in the Kunsthistorisches Museum,
Vienna. His work has passed beyond the religious subject ; he is the
most modern of the artists working in Venice at that time. The church
is simply a place. Feelings reminiscent of religion come and go, suggested by the flick of a wave, the gleam of a sail in the distance, a
storm suddenly sketched, a trembling quality in the *palazzi* on the
Grand Canal. Buildings, boats, men are of the same element as the
water, ruffled, about to break up, only a breath away from the in-
visible energy that brought them into being ; a world without roots,
its space and its time illusions.

As for the famous couple of canvases, *Il Ridotto* and *Il Parlatorio*,
in the Ca' Rezzonico, they are attributed to Francesco and/or his
brother Gian Antonio at will. The *ridotto* is that of S. Moisè : the
coffee counter can be seen in a further room ; the floor is strewn with
cards ; there are musicians ; a patrician is recognised by his having no
mask. If we look quickly from this to the *Parlatorio* on the other side
of the room we shall notice a certain ease of tone in the latter, a
smoothness and assurance that may mean more Francesco than Gian
Antonio for us. The picture shows heavily jewelled girls behind the
convent grille, entertaining their guests. There is a beggar and a cripple.
This is the *parlatorio* of the S. Zaccaria convent, near St Mark's Square.
To support the choice of Francesco, a sketch on the same subject
said to be by him is in the Museo Correr. And a sketch for the *ridotto*
by Gian Antonio exists in the Art Institute of Chicago.

It seemed as if no Venetian artist could resist giving some record
of Venice, but Canaletto went further in a stone-by-stone record than
anyone else, as if he knew that his was the last real Venice. In fact,
his record is so clear and precise that it has never been of great interest
to Venetians. Yet his careful records were still within a Venetian

tradition started by Gentile Bellini. If we want to know how little matter-of-fact his work really was we only have to look at some of his imitators – Vincenzo Chilone's *View of the Pool of St Mark*, for instance ; it shows how studied and unfeeling a record can become. All Canaletto's views are diffused with a certain easy light, something that pulls them delicately away from being simply physical views. *St Mark's Square*, done in 1723 (now in Lugano) gives us a glimpse of the Basilica with market stalls before it, without figures almost ; the surfaces are rendered so carefully that it is like a re-building of them. His *View of the Grand Canal* has long gondolas sweeping from one side to the other, seeming to try to fly out of the water, while a shadow falls on the still water from the palaces. It is quite different from Francesco Guardi's impressionist glance. *The Grand Canal with the Church of the Carità* (1726) shows the church elongated, part of its wall sharp in the light, almost bizarre, hanging over the canal, casting a deep shadow, and half in shadow itself. It is easy to see Canaletto's views as simple records, but they convey a reflective pause, inside which every stone and wave are fixed. His *Piazzetta* (with its view of Sta Maria della Salute on the other side of the Canal) and his *S. Cristoforo della Pace and S. Michele* in the lagoon, seen from the Fondamenta Nuove (both in the British Royal Collection), have a sheen of utter calm, a silence that becomes the actual constitution of the stones and the distant cupolas, even the standing figures. And his other view of *Sta Maria della Salute*, from a closer angle, makes that self-assertive building as thin and fragile as a pencil drawing ; this coincides with our experience too – the Canal and the sky have a trick of turning that unsightly mass of stone, gaping across the Canal's mouth towards the public gardens, into something as light as air. Even in strikingly realistic pictures like *The Carità seen from the Marble Works of S. Vitale*, in the National Gallery, London, we find a moment caught in its depth, without movement, fixed for always, with its hot and blinding sunshine in the foreground, and its shadowy water beyond. Sometimes, his detail does go to a point of too fine an observation, and the scene loses its atmosphere. *The Portico of the Procuratie Nuove and the Florian Café*, also in the National Gallery, gives most of its attention to the portico's curved ceiling and its hanging lamps, to the pillars and the wall of the Campanile, to the little turrets, arches and steeples of the Basilica; it is one of his few pictures which really feature people. Sometimes the desire to set the ecstasy down, to make a record, became so strong that it ended in an inventory. That was why Guardi chose to do what seems at first sight a sketch.

By the time we reach Tiepolo's son Gian Domenico at the end of the eighteenth century (his work is generously attributed to his father by almost everyone) we have a suggestion of the grotesque, a hint of mockery which was quite unknown before. There had always been a layer of cynicism under patrician life; now, with the galloping power of French fashions, which brought in not only dazzling new styles of clothes but a hard sophistication, it began to destroy the old sweet intimacy. Goldoni's *La Villeggiatura* parodies the imported ideas: Don Paoluccio, Donna Lavinia's *cicisbeo*, is just back from Paris, and almost nothing he says fails to mention the fact. '*O Francia felicissima in questo!*' – 'You can't bear France on *that* subject!'. If you love someone, he says, you must never show it; the great thing now is indifference – '*Pompa si fa dell'indifferenza!*'. He has seen through the whole farce of *cicisbeism*: does Donna Lavinia *really* love him? has she *really* missed him? He certainly hasn't missed her; while he hesitates to say this, he gives her to understand it. And to the woman he does acknowledge as his lover he says, '*Vi servo coll'animo. Il cuore è vostro. Addio, madama, non mi ricercate di più*': 'I serve you with my soul. My heart is yours. Goodbye, madam, don't come near me again!'. It is a delightful stroke: he must end, and does, by reducing himself to a 'little Paul' without feelings and therefore of no further interest to the women. When any society becomes ashamed of its intimacy it falters. The new fashion, whether it was really Parisian or not, ate steadily into the patrician class, and cut them off for the first time from their own people. And ironically this new aristocratic import from France was the vehicle by which French revolutionary ideas came in.

Too many people were too corrupt by now for grace and intimacy to survive. In Domenico Tiepolo there is nothing astringent or cruel. But nothing counts any more. He gives us views of the sky, like his father's views, but it is all a joke: a rope is slung across the open spaces above and a *pulcinella* balances on it, his long cap and thin, protruding nose like a last mocking – but also sad and perplexed – gesture to the empty sky. And we find that we are looking up not from the roof of the world, as we always were in his father's pieces, but from a deep hole in the ground. The *pulcinella* is balancing over the mouth of the hole ; only *he* is in the world, on its surface, while we are in the dark bowels of the earth.

Even in Domenico's *The New World* (all these can be seen in the Ca' Rezzonico) there is no straight record of a daily event, nothing even like a serious satire. The spectators of the 'New World' (an open-air show of cardboard panoramas, popular in Venice) are grotesque, though the painter gives no deliberate sign that he thinks so ; they simply are ; there is something futile in the way they all stand there. We see Domenico himself on the right, holding his hat ; his wigged father stands in front of him. These two are a little separate: they are the only real spectators, looking at the rest of them.

His clowns are almost monsters in the way they point and huddle together, and sit hunched, speechless and still, as if they were the last people on the earth ; these places are silent, deserted. What are they pointing at ? We look: nothing. That is their joke too. So much has been played with, so many feelings have been exploited to squeeze the last drops of pleasure, so much folly has been exposed, that there seems no point in being serious about anything any more.

In *The Dance* there is no real dance: the *cicisbeo* holds his lady by the hand, one foot lifted in a strange movement, unctuous and yet self-assured, almost mocking ; she has a tall hat like a pillow-case and an immense bustle. His *Clowns* really are dancing, the female holding a fan with fatuous ease while the male closes his hand over one of her breasts ; but they are not real clowns ; they are only in carnival dress ; they are perhaps what the lady and her *cicisbeo* are underneath. Perhaps Gian Domenico's finest, certainly his strangest piece of work is the *Passeggiata Invernale*, showing two women in a winter scene simply gazing towards us, one hidden behind her fan except for two still eyes, grave, watching, unattached. The world is empty. We are on the edge of the romantic.

Chapter 7

A Dying Nobility
and a Healthy People

Venice, unlike other Italian towns, had the equivalent of divorce, only it was called annulment; and what people called divorce was in fact legal separation. Independence from Rome meant more annulments than elsewhere: between 1782 and 1796 the Ten registered two hundred and sixty-four applications and most of them were granted. This seems small until we remember the size of the patrician class. The reason lay in the fact that husbands and wives no longer shared a function: if they now took little interest in their children it was because the family name meant nothing in terms of state power. The glow of names like Giustiniani, Loredan, Sagredo, Pisani was no longer sustained by great actions. The man was no longer a hard-worked servant of the state, since the state itself was idle, and the woman was therefore no longer a symbol of the honour of her house; they were both bent on pleasure, night and day; there was little else to spend their great energies or wealth on.

But among the common people the family remained intact, simply because its function survived: there was too little money for pleasure night and day. Therefore they were in a way the more prosperous of the two classes, inside the limits of their wants. And their continuing health kept the state going as long as it did, just as it made the survival of the city possible during first the French and then the long Austrian occupations. The ordinary people were healthy: the women were freer than ever before but their pleasures were systematic. They formed clubs and spent the funds on little day-trips, leaving the men behind; it was thought rather indecent for women to enjoy themselves in front of the men, so strong were the surviving influences of that Islamic rigour which had once governed all Venetian family life. Two elderly men were sent along with them as a kind of nominal protection ; they had a picnic and danced together (mostly the *villota*, a country hop), then they made a tired journey home in a boat lit with coloured lanterns, mooring at the *fondamenta* where their men were waiting.

A people peacefully at work, whatever deportations or sudden arrests or official murders in the night were going on, had been the Venetian rule for nearly a thousand years. A more sweetly disposed population could not be found in Europe : every visitor remarked on it. And the eighteenth century was a climax of kindly manners.

There was a serene regularity of daily life. The church-bells rang the *mattutin* an hour before sunrise, when the guards were taken off the Piazza and the ducal palace ; then St Mark's enormous bell, called the *marangona*, sounded a *mezza terza* or half-third to mark the dawn, and this drew everyone to work or to Mass. The food-shops were open about half an hour before sunrise. Not only the working people were about at this hour : the patricians were at their offices by tierce (eight o'clock in the summer and ten o'clock in winter), and stayed there until one o'clock, when they were free to enjoy themselves. Most working people left off work at sundown, when the bell called the *realtina* (belonging to the church of S. Giovanni di Rialto) sounded. Shops closed about nine in the evening, as they tend to still in Italy today, but many of the food-shops were open until midnight, when the *marangona* sounded again, this time sixteen-in-eighteen.

Most of the business of the city took place at or near the Rialto with its daily fair, and also in St Mark's Square, where all kinds of velvet and brocade and damask were on display : as today, the Rialto was the place for deals, the Square for expensive buying. There were about twenty-five bread shops in the city ; at the quay there were the mint and the public granaries and the fish-stalls. Fish carts did a daily round of the *calle* : with the permanent fish-market on the Grand Canal this made a vast daily supply, and hungry fish-eating was necessarily a strong tradition. Boats brought fruit and vegetables from the islands, and landed them near the Palazzo Camerlenghi, by the Rialto bridge.

At dawn anyone sleeping on the Grand Canal was woken by a

massive din, and if they looked out of their windows they saw the whole water apparently covered with fruit and vegetables, on one raft or barge after another so close together that hardly a wave was visible between them. That was how Venice's food arrived. 'I am persuaded,' said Mrs Thrale, 'if one were to live here (which would not be for long, I think), he should forget the use of sleep, what with the market folks bringing up the boats from *terra firma* loaded with every produce of nature, neatly arranged in these flat-bottomed conveyances, the coming up of which begins about three o'clock in a morning and ends about six ; the gondoliers rowing home their masters about that hour, and so on till eight ; the common business of the town, which it is then time to begin.' But she found the 'morning amusements interesting . . . the street orators and the mountebanks in the square, the shops and stalls where chickens and ducks were sold by auction under the hammer'. And she enjoyed the food – 'such fish waits one's knife and fork as I most certainly did never see before, and as I suppose are not to be seen in any sea but this in such perfection. Fresh sturgeon (*ton*, as they call it), and fresh anchovies, large as herrings, and dressed like sprats in London, incomparable ; turbots, like those of Torbay exactly, and plentiful as there, with enormous pipers, are what one principally eats here. The fried liver, without which an Italian can hardly go from day to day, is so charmingly dressed as at Milan, that I grew to like it as well as they ; but at Venice it is sad stuff, and they call it *fegao*.'

There was a 'wine-bank' or Riva del Vin by the Rialto where the wine-boats moored, as they do today. The city tinkled, throbbed, hummed and sang from dawn on : its day sped along briskly and joyfully, the city being so old, so established in its habits, that everyone found his system of life ready for him, so to speak. Children played *lippa* or skittles in the narrow *calli*. Water was drawn from the wells in clanking buckets. 'They sing in the squares, in the streets, along the canals,' Goldoni said. 'The merchants sing while offering their goods ; the workers sing on their way home from work ; the gondoliers sing while they wait for their masters.' By the eighteenth century the singing had become sweet and languorous. If Goethe was right, the

F

gondoliers still remembered their Tasso, and sang it from one side of the lagoon to the other, exchanging verse for verse, stirring people almost to madness. A famous gondolier-singer was Giovanni Sibillato, who ended as a courier for the ministry of health. He accompanied himself on the guitar and was asked to perform in noble houses. Another was doge Grimani's personal gondolier, Antonio Bianchi: but some people say that the doge and other noblemen wrote his verses for him.

At night each *calle* had a lamp, perhaps two, and link-boys or *codege* lighted people from place to place, their lamps lit by the *impizzaferai*, whose job was as defined and sacred as that of the ragged old men on the Molo who hooked in the boats with strange crooks studded with coins and little bronze figures. Real street-lamps were brought in about 1732 and eighteenth-century Venice became one of the best-lit towns in the peninsula, though the *codege*, sacred as before, remained. As for the policemen, there were mainly two kinds – the *bombardieri* (the equivalent of the modern *carabinieri*) and the *sbirri* or street constables (whose nearest equivalent today is perhaps the *vigile*). Then there was the dreaded special agent of the Ten who could wake you in the night and search your house – the *Missier Grande*, whose men were like Mussolini's *Questura*, designed for the surveillance of private life. But nothing was easier than quieting a Venetian mob: it is questionable if mobs in the real sense ever existed in Venice. The police, even the special agents, were respected, and it was said of the last agent there ever was, just before the fall of the Republic, that the sight of him in the square was enough to stop any disorder. When the Russian Grand Duke Paul Petrovitch visited Venice only three policemen were found necessary in the Square during the whole of the celebrations, which went on night and day. Venetian order had never been reduced to law: it lay in the people themselves, a healthy good sense derived from sound government, from plenty of work and higher living standards than anywhere else on the mainland. Being themselves common people, part of the family, the police were kindly, gay, easy-tempered. The murder in a side-alley after dark, though much talked about outside Venice, happened rarely: scuffles and pranks were more frequent, and the police used their truncheons, but there was never violence in the modern sense, no viciousness of feeling. And there was less robbery than in any town in Italy. The number of murders in one year never exceeded twenty, and was nearer three or four, against Rome's annual average of a thousand (in the eleven years of Pope Clement XIII's reign there were over twelve thousand). Gondoliers always shouted and cursed, they raised their oars against each other and yelled elaborate insults until their voices could no longer be heard, but there was hardly ever fighting. The word for 'yes' in Venice was always 'at your service'.

Until the seventeenth century the people had been hardy and self-denying. Then softening – and sensualising – influences worked on the people as on the nobles. French fashions brought in a new lightness of touch – in wit, in the behaviour of women, as well as in clothes: Venetian women had never been skittish before. But still the family remained intact. Everybody was proud to be Venetian, both the 'tabarro', or ordinary citizen, and the 'toga', or nobleman.

One key to the well-being of the work-people was the fact that the government always saw to it that they never worked too hard, and that no child was employed beyond its powers. Girls were exploited in the lace-industry, but then long hours with little pay seems to have been the practice for nubile girls everywhere in Italy, and persists today. On holidays Venice stopped work by law, and there were plenty of holidays. Wine-shops, chemists, cafés and some of the bread-shops remained open. And everyone went to church – another reason for the well-being. Nobody thought that life ended with death – an idea more depressant of vigour and serenity than any known to the mind. Even with the flood of free-thinking ideas from France there was no serious undermining of a vague but deep religious sense; even Casanova believed in God, and prayed all his life.

And of course a people whose carnival goes on for six months of the year must have *some* happiness to celebrate. The mask became Venice's passport to pleasure. It personified a mysterious quality that she had always had: something that seemed to whisper from the sea, winding its way round buildings, at your side in the alleys, lying flat and dazzling out in the lagoon, its air seeping through your closed bed-curtains at night. The appearance of the sea at every corner was always her strangest secret, bringing a reminder of infinity wherever one went, floating one drowsily from place to place, its light changing every hour. Venice is never simply another human city, simply mortal, here and now. And the carnival mask seemed to complete that sweet cancelling-out of the finite human creature, locked in his space and time; he became almost an element like the sea. Really the mask-habit swamped Venetian life. It took away every barrier there had been. Working girls could sit next to patrician women at the gambling tables and lose what fortune they had. Perhaps only in the eighteenth century did Venice achieve a daily life proper to herself: as if the mood of the sea, that had lapped against the *fondamenti* and the palace steps for so many centuries, won through at last, removing ambition, even passion, and saying like Monteverdi's Apollo, '*Troppo, troppo gioisti Di tua lieta ventura ; Or troppo piangi Tua sorte acerba a dura*' – 'You were far too joyful in good fortune, as you now mourn too much your hard and bitter fate'.

Carnival began on St Stephen's day, 26 December, when permission to wear masks was given publicly by a government-officer dressed in odd pantomime clothes, in St Mark's Square. The ensemble of the black or white mask covering most of the face, with the *bauta*, a hood of velvet or silk over the shoulders and the rest of the head, under a three-cornered hat, looked sombre only to visitors: under it every woman was a *zentildonna*, class and even sex were cancelled out, and everyone became a secret spectator. Even servants wore masks when they went shopping. Even beggars used them. During the masquerades patricians and ordinary citizens crowded together round the triumphal carriages and threaded their way through the *calli* singing and dancing.

The wildest day was Maundy Thursday, when fireworks were let off in the Piazza in broad daylight, and a bull was beheaded by members of the Smiths' and Butchers' guilds, in fantastic costumes. A rope was slung between the top of the Campanile and the doge's box by the four bronze horses, and an acrobat performed the annual *volo* or flight, to present a bouquet to the doge when he touched down. Eggs were flung about (not bad ones, but full of perfumed water) by a carnival character called Mattacino, who wore a feathered hat and looked like a chicken. Pantaloon, Zanni with his stockings that were always too wide, Brighella, Doctor Graziano and Doctor Balanzon, both dressed like university professors in black and reciting endless grotesque speeches that made no sense, were seen everywhere in the crowds. There was Harlequin with his tar face and many-coloured tunic, his hat with a hare's fud in it. There were the 'Calabrians' playing their pipes, the *guaghi* – men dressed as women. There were puppet-shows, fortune-tellers, wandering musicians singing to the guitar, there were quacks and perfumiers. Wild beasts were displayed behind bars ; in fact, the rhinoceros of the 1751 carnival caused so much excitement that Longhi painted his portrait, and people talked about him for the next half-century. In 1784 a gas-balloon was sent up, one year after the famous Montgolfier brothers had made a successful flight in France.

After six months of it the celebrations roared to a sudden full stop : there were red flares and rockets, a mass of masked and painted and costumed people dancing and joining hands ; fireworks went up continuously, and fell with a thrilling hiss into the water ; the shouting, the beating of drums, the laughter and squeals of pleasure were such that the city seemed to tremble ; sweets, oranges, ribbons, pumpkin seeds and confetti were trampled on the paving stones. At midnight the *marangona* and the bell of S. Francesco della Vigna tolled slowly, and by dawn there was only the coloured trash in the streets, and an unusually complete silence, with Venice's typical night-sounds, the lapping of water on stone and the slight boom of boats on their moorings.

The favourite game to watch, especially for the working people, was the fist-fight (*pugni*), but over the centuries it had so often gone too far that by the middle of the eighteenth century the government had forbidden it. Everyone loved the game called the 'forces of Hercules' which replaced these long battles : a number of naked gondoliers formed two lines facing each other, usually on boats strung together ; planks were put between them, on their shoulders, and another group of men mounted the planks ; another group mounted on these, and so on until a great human tier was formed, crowned by a child on top.

The planks often tumbled down, with the whole of the group, into the water. The game was usually played near the Rialto. It was fun, and less cruel than the popular bull-baiting.

Each of Venice's parishes celebrated its patron saint with a *sagra* or fête, when carpets were hung from windows and flags mounted in the streets. There was much dancing, with the women in special costumes, bouquets behind their ears ; a lot of it was too wild to be called dancing – more a hearty burlesque. The women spun round and round so that their skirts whirled to waist level, while others made mock-erotic movements to the sound of the drum, the fife, the guitar, the tambourine. Burlesque was understood at once, a recognized style of humour in all classes. In the second half of the eighteenth century a mock regatta of wheelbarrows was held at the Rialto, sometimes at Sta Maria di Formosa ; they were raced along with an uproarious clatter, and the prize was wine. There was burlesque too in the ceremony of 'the old woman' during canival, when mock honours were paid to an effigy by a pair of attendants. Then the effigy was sawn in half to the sound of drums, crackers were tied to the feet of dogs and the masked 'old woman' was burned.

On Easter Monday everybody turned out to see the *fresco*, or procession of gondolas, which was repeated every Sunday and holiday from that time until September. The boats were denuded of their *felze*, and the patricians in them could be seen by everyone ; thousands of these *gondole al fresco* filed down the Grand Canal from Sta Lucia (or what is now the railway station) to the Piazzetta at the other end. The gala costume of the *gondolieri di casada* or house-gondoliers was very striking and gay – a red sash round the waist, a red cap, white shoes, and a silk jacket and stockings. On the evening of a regatta there was always great gaiety. The houses of the winners were hung with garlands, and their doors were left open ; the silk flag of victory was hung in the local *campo* for everyone to see, and there was a late supper with lots of singing and dancing.

The wine-shops (called *magazzeni*) were a favourite meeting place for ordinary people, the equivalent of the casino. *Furatole* were pork-butchers where wine was drunk. If we see many *calli* and *campi* in

Venice today with the name of 'Malvasia' it is because of the pre-
valence of shops where foreign wines used to be served, among them
the Malvasian wine Epirus, sometimes called *grecchetto*, and which we
would call malmsey. The sweeter variety was preferred by the
Venetian, and was actually called 'enjoyment' – *garba*. As in the
modern Italian *cantina* the benches and tables were of rough wood ;
the wine was served from an earthenware bowl called the *mezzo
boccaleto* (or 'little half-mouth') which always sat in the middle of the
table. Sometimes the tavern-keepers turned pawnbroker and gave
specially bad wine (called *vin da pegni* or 'pawn-wine') plus a little
cash in return for goods. Another place to go was the *latteria*, where
you sat and drank milk or ate whipped cream with wafers, a habit
which survives only in some mainland villages today. The *latterie*
were called *pestrini* in Venice, perhaps from the word *pestare* 'to beat
or pound' (our own word 'pestle' derives from it), an allusion to the
whipped cream. If these places were popular they were never exclusive :
all classes mingled in them – in the *malvasie*, the ordinary wine-shops,
in the pork-butchers and the milk-shops. They were the down-town
haunts, so to speak, of the young bloods.

Eating was always moderate in Venice, but it got careful attention :
on Christmas Eve salmon and eels were eaten with cabbage ; the last
day of the carnival meant rissoles and turkey and whipped cream, the
first day of Lent lentils ; lamb was for Easter, duck for the first of
August. Even noblemen ate their elaborate and often sickly French
dishes only at the great banquets, and then mostly for the show of it.
There was probably greater variety in the Venetian kitchen than anywhere else in the peninsula, due to the continual influx of foreigners
and the influence of Greece and the Levant. Venice is the only place
in Italy today where hot curry dishes, tempered with slices of baked
polenta, are served as a matter of course.

A remarkable sanity prevailed among the Venetians because they
were governed like one big family. Unfaithful wives were banished
or kept at home under a sort of house-arrest, cuckolded husbands were
warned by the government about the size of their horns. Like the decrees condemning extravagance, this vigilance only had a curbing

effect: the wives went on cuckolding if they really wanted to, and husbands bore their horns with frivolity. But vigilance was all that was necessary to secure a continuing state of sound health. People knew they could not go too far, whatever class they came from: when a loud scandal started, whether in one of the grand palaces along the Canal or in a tiny house of the Canareggio district, the government stepped in with quiet warnings. In 1731 a young count was declared an outlaw together with the girl he had run away with. It was never enough in Venice simply to look after your interests: you had to watch the interests of the city as well. That was why you never saw a drunkard on the streets. And this sobriety survives in the Venetian of today: a friendly scuffle even between students will cause an involuntary look of mute disapproval, as if a law of sound good sense had been broken. Sobriety survived the carnival every year because the pleasure was never of the dissipated kind; perhaps no society in Christendom ever defined pleasure so well, by grounding it on sound health. Montesquieu and a good many other foreigners found them morally the healthiest people in Europe.

The mistaken English surgeon, Dr Sharp, whom Giuseppe Baretti disliked so much, said that it was quite common for a man and his lover to have a tête-à-tête all night at the casino, after flirting at the opera in his box, and for them to go to Mass (supposedly having made love) on the way home in the morning. Nothing so grossly simple ever took place in Venice. People were interested in more than the simple act of fornication. Only for someone born in a northern society did so much grace necessarily end up in bed. The fear of scandal and the impossibility of real secrecy for long kept the women to heel; and family traditions, more powerful than anywhere north of the Alps, kept a bare skeleton of the old chastity. Anyone like Casanova who never enjoyed sleeping alone (even in the afternoon) could find endless adventures in all classes; but so he could have, and did, anywhere in Europe or on the Italian mainland. What made the foreigners goggle in Venice was the love that everyone carried on their sleeves, which softened nearly every woman's face and voice and movements.

The debauchery of the noble class was at worst late nights and too

....

The Venetians of G. D. Tiepolo
OPPOSITE The minuet
OVERLEAF Scenes from Venetian life

much coffee. As they did little or no work their recuperation was swift. The rich merchants aped them, let their wives copy their fashions and hold banquets and continually endanger their health and wealth, but they did it in loyalty to the oligarchy of great families above them (they looked on them as the only people fit to govern), not for the ends of pleasure, much less debauchery. When Napoleon suppressed the monasteries and foreclosed the mortgages they had granted to noblemen, he destroyed the patrician class in a flash, because they had to sell out at cruelly low rates: but the only people he pleased, apart from the criminal types among the ordinary people, were the poor nobles, the *Barnabotti*, who now saw their masters their equals. Even the professional middle class – the Secretaries who sat at the meetings of the Ten and the Inquisitors and the Senate – did not share this social resentment: having more and more say in government policy as the century went on, they were as happy as the people. The middle class – all those with money and no blue blood – led a stricter life than the nobles, but then they considered that as merchants they ought to: their women mostly did without *cicisbei*, and like the ordinary people they enjoyed a tranquil family life. But they were aware of the very rich (no Venetian could fail to be, with so many fêtes and banquets and stupendous costly extravaganzas for foreign princes); and naturally some of the debauchery trickled down. But debauchery was not what brought Venice down: its fall came as a stupendous surprise even to those who had predicted it.

The most stoutly patriotic group among the common people, radiating pride and vigour, had always been the *Arsenalotti* or the Arsenal workers. They were incorruptible, as the Genoese had found out centuries before. When great fires broke out they were always called. During two in the sixteenth century they saved most of the ducal palace; both times they refused payment from the doge, though they did accept a dinner date from him (which, seeing that there were fifteen hundred of them, cost him very much more). They were expected to be as efficient and healthy as a little army, which was why they had fencing classes and did gymnastics. Three *provveditori* lived in palazzi inside the Arsenal; at least one of them had to be on duty

A visit to the moneylender
The execution of Pulcinello

at any time. They built Venice's ships, defended its harbour, manned the life-boats. The collapse of patriotism in this quarter was perhaps the most symptomatic thing that happened to eighteenth-century Venice. It is interesting that Venetians today date their present decline (for the first time in their history the protective shelves of land are breaking down from lack of adequate repair) to the closing of the Arsenal about fifteen years after the last war, when eleven thousand families had to leave.

Pride in the guilds or *scuole* had always been the most passionate collective feeling among the ordinary people. On the island of Murano, glass manufacture brought into being not only a class of specialists with their own privileges, but a virtually independent little republic with its *nuncio* in Venice and the power to run its own trials outside the jurisdiction of Venice's *Missier Grande*. Murano even had a minia-ture doge, called the *Podestà*, who lacked personal freedom in precisely the same way as the doge of Venice lacked it : he had to be a nobleman, but he could not interfere in local affairs ; he had to be in Murano at least three days out of four, and he was kept on the island whenever an important function was taking place in Venice. Apart from the charters belonging to their particular trades of glass-blowing, bead-making, glass-staining and so on – the workers too had a Golden Book of their own, in which one hundred and seventy-three families were inscribed, out of a population of thirty thousand ; and this local nobility was a technical one, including the highest practitioners from the various guilds. A master glass-blower's daughter was once allowed to marry a Venetian nobleman, and the names of their children were written in Venice's Golden Book.

Specialized work in Venice drew wealth from every part of the world, and was protected from competition by steep import duties. Wages were good, food-prices low. Only the lace-industry – the finest in the world by far – lacked a proper corporation, and its products were sold by middlemen for many times the price received by the women. Louis XIV is said to have worn a rose-point collar from Venice at his coronation. For this design no white thread existed that was fine enough, and white hair had to be used. Like the glass-blowers, the lace-makers were under constant beguilement to go abroad, particularly to France: the penalty of emigration was pursuit by the Venetian stiletto and punishment for the rest of the family if they stayed behind. But this did not stop Muranese workers drifting into the service of the Duke of Buckingham, and at the end of the seventeenth century others had taken the secret of the Venetian mirror to France. Lace-workers slipped away to France with their world-famous *punto di Venezia*; a lace factory based on Venetian labour was started at Rheims by a nun, as a monopoly. The industry moved to England and Belgium, and the new factories even sent their work back to Venice to be sold. In the eighteenth century there was a great fling of craftsmanship, as if, in the absence of the old glories, the genius of the people had to make a last conquest: their taste was known everywhere, exquisite and unerring, natural and spontaneous.

Venice's cloth, lace, furniture, metalwork, tapestry, pottery were talked about all over Europe. The smallest items – keys, snuff-boxes, ink-pots, candlesticks – had a quite distinctive grace. The city burst with talent. The velvets, the colth of gold and the silks on sale at the *Merceria*, were the finest you could buy. And there were commodities from every part of the world, especially from the Levant and the Far East, to keep taste alive and new designs frequent. 'Upon my return to Venice,' William Beckford said, 'I found myself able to thread its labyrinth of streets, canals and alleys, in search of amber and oriental curiosities. The variety of exotic merchandise, the perfume of coffee, the shade of awnings, and the sight of Greeks and Asiatics sitting cross-legged under them, made me think myself in the bazaars of Constantinople.'

Only towards the end of the century did Venetian work become shoddy and clearly inferior to foreign goods – when her international and maritime position had collapsed, and she had become part of the Italian mainland for the first time.

Chapter 8

La Zentildonna

Being a woman in Venice was a profession. She had to set the Serenissima off, be its pride and consolation; a woman changed according to the state of the Republic and the male tastes that happened to prevail. Whether these corresponded to her own choice, much less her own happiness, had no importance. It was a wonder that a clever woman could survive in Venice: but there were a few, especially in the eighteenth century when she was a pleasure-symbol and no longer the remote doll she had been a century before, strutting along on stilts, the bearer of family prestige and talking to no one. She was beguiling now, with *'occhio lascivo in ziro e seducente, sedizioso el parlar, sia brute o bele'* – 'a roaming, lascivious, seductive eye, seditious in speech, whether plain or beautiful'. But then she was freer than ever before. Venice now required her freedom. She too was free to fall.

The liberation of patrician women from a strait and secluded home-life began during the sixteenth century with the coming of opulent standards. Young patrician girls had once been forbidden the licence of going to church on Sundays, ever since 1482 when a young man whisked off a girl called Giovanna di Riviera on her way to church and married her outside Venetian territory; after that Mass was celebrated at home, in the private chapel. A wife had once lived little more than a harem existence, under the same roof with Circassian and Giorgian women, slaves with whom she shared her husband and who often meant more to him than she did. She went out rarely, and when she did was under heavy chaperonage; in the period of luxury her high clogs secured the same effect, though she did go out more. Even her children were taken from her early, the boys to serve their seniors in the Great Council, running messages, bringing coffee and carrying the ballot boxes with their golden and silver balls, the girls to close their minds to all but daily trivialities in a convent.

In the earlier epochs social life had not been open to women. The only time they had been expected to appear in public was on state occasions, as part of the patrician parade, and even then they had been closely hemmed in with family. In other parts of Italy women led nowhere near such an Eastern life, a fact which makes the rapid abandonment of discipline in the last two centuries of the Republic even more remarkable. By the end of that time what Italians call 'the equilateral triangle' (wife, husband and lover) was, if not established, not something to be surprised at. But then foreign influences had intruded. No one was surprised in London that the fifth Duke of Devonshire lived in a smooth triangle with his wife Georgiana and her friend Lady Elizabeth Foster. By that time the patricians everywhere in Europe had common habits: Georgiana, like many of the Venetian women, was if anything more interested in the card-table than love.

The height and costliness of the clog was a measure of sexual morality. In the sixteenth century it had reached its highest and most expensive; the Sumptuary Laws imposed a fine of twenty-five lire for clogs beyond the allowed measurements or of too elaborate design. Fine pearls were forbidden as a form of decoration, and even the permitted embroidery could not be too rich. These shoes lasted as a form of patrician display, though there was nothing in the rest of Europe like them, until the end of the seventeenth century. And then – with the disappearance of heroes and Mediterranean hegemony – they went out so thoroughly that women seemed to have no shoes at all.

Middle-class women, on the other hand, had a much better time before the eighteenth century, and what became the fashionable salons where men and women not only mixed but actually talked seriously (though on mostly frivolous subjects) were really a refinement of middle-class gatherings. Even the tradition of the *cicisbeo* may have been of middle-class origin, at least in Venice: as early as the sixteenth century it was possible for a burgher's wife to allow herself a little feeling towards another man than her husband, though in an Arcadian way. Compared with her the patrician woman lived a lonely prisoner at home and a puppet outside, wobbling on her clogs under a head-dress so loaded with jewellery and flowers that she could hardly raise her head.

The freest women of all had naturally been the courtesans, who supplied noblemen with anything they wanted after their Giorgian slave-women and their wives had finished with them : they offered sex with wit and Arcadian pleasantries, which no wife was literate or free enough to do, while the slave-women sometimes spoke no Italian. There were eleven thousand, six hundred and fifty-four courtesans at the end of the sixteenth century (someone actually counted them and listed their addresses in a book), an astonishing number for a population that fluctuated between a hundred thousand and a hundred and fifty thousand ; they numbered ten times the patrician wives, and nearly ten times the burgher wives. Unlike the women of any other class they could mix freely with men in the highest places. During Henri III's visit the most famous courtesan of the day, Veronica Franco, fell in love with him at once ; she never slept with another man as long as she lived ; in fact, she withdrew from social life and tried to get other courtesans to do the same. Money and lavish apartments, clothes and jewellery were showered on them ; they were nicely graded according to their beauty and grace of speech, which meant a hierarchy of price as well as social eminence.

It is clear that eighteenth-century Venice required *all* her women to be courtesans ; and the result was that there was no sweeter breed of woman in Europe. Président de Brosses, who made love to seven or eight of them, said he did not believe that 'fairies and angels combined' could have produced beauties like them.

The punishment for elopement or even for sleeping with another man was no longer the death-penalty, but then neither was the prize a Grand Duchy as it had been for the wicked Bianca Capello who eloped from Venice with a bank-clerk in the sixteenth-century. In 1705 Rosalba did a priceless little portrait of a girl holding a fluttering bird : her mouth is ever so slightly open in a smile, she is casually dressed ; there is nothing on her head ; she holds the bird with a soft, unconcentrated grasp, as if giving all her attention to the painter, her great black eyes shining slightly, dreaming into the distance. It argues only grace – no discipline, or even the expectation of it any more. And grace, not family honour, is what the men look for. The woman is now their delighted servant. This little girl was the product of centuries of admiring envy for the courtesans, endured in closed rooms, with the Giorgian woman singing below. In the eighteenth century she broke into action.

But it was no real liberation. She was fussed over and complimented and praised and combed and escorted in an endless titillation that must have stirred her desires without always giving her the means of satisfying them. For whatever else Venice was, it was not a whore-house.

The change that really came about was her entry into public life. Everything she had known until then took place in the family, and for many it still did. As soon as a girl became engaged she put on a mask and was not seen publicly until after her marriage. Then, some people say, she became the common property of her husband and his brothers, especially when only the senior male of the family married ; it at least ensured that if there were mistakes, the child would be of the same blood. That was how close-knit a family was in Venice : it meant that the patrician women who slept with their *cicisbei* were rare.

Betrothal was still a special rite, extending over many days and culminating in as extravagant a wedding as possible. The marriages were still nearly all arranged, in the middle class as well, but the couple were nowadays given more chance to see each other before the wedding day. In the first few days of the engagement the young man walked up and down under his future bride's window, at certain expected times, to serenade her. Then he would be allowed in the house to see her for the first time and give her the little betrothal ring, called the *ricordino*, or memento. A few days before the wedding she would get a pearl necklace from her mother, in a special ceremony which could be seen by friends of the family. She would then visit Venice's convents in a gondola, the floor of its cabin spread with a magnificent carpet. When she went to her future husband's house for the first time she was led into the hall by the *ballerino* or dancing master of the family, dressed in black. It was here that the wedding took place, under the family chaplain, and the guests shouted 'Kiss! Kiss!' to the couple at the end of the ceremony. The bride danced alone in a single performance before the assembly, and she was then escorted through the house by a male guest. The banquet began, followed by dancing until the early hours; and celebrations went on for two or three days afterwards. And, according to temperament and family tradition, the couple either became intimate with each other or simply went through the mechanics of marriage for the production of children and barely spoke to each other again. If they found they hated each other they could get a legal separation ('divorce'), though the best solution was an annulment, as it meant you could marry again, this time without having your partner chosen for you. In either case a petition had to be addressed to the Ten, but no great difficulties were involved if you were patrician and powerful. Usually the wife sued for divorce, on the grounds of cruelty, unless there was a mutual agreement to separate. But on the whole marriages remained intact, and women of every class were remarkably dutiful.

Once a patrician woman had gone through her first pearl-wearing year she chose her *cicisbeo*, and it was a disgrace for her – and her husband – not to have one. He must be of the same rank as herself, have been in the Senate and the councils of state, a man of such influence that he could serve her family politically at any time. That of course was on the highest level. Once it had been arranged she could do what she liked, or what her husband liked. The French ambassador once remarked ironically to the Président de Brosses that on the whole the *cicisbei* did not sleep with their women – he knew no more than fifty who did.

The word *cicisbeo* comes from *cicisbeare*, or *bisbigliare* as the Italians now say, meaning to whisper, as lovers do. The tradition was a very old one. All 'polite' Italians imbibed chivalrous ideas in early childhood, and the sacredness of women was planted in their minds, though it might not mean the sacredness of the women they shared house with. It was an idea, a vision. If today a woman's voice can shame an Italian man better than any policeman's, it is on account of that long-sustained tradition. Looking at anything beautiful raises your mind to the universal of beauty : that was the platonic idea, and the basis of chivalry. The woman represents love ; she is its image. In 1214 a castle of Love was erected at Treviso, and all Venice went there : the women defended their castle with roses, perfumed waters, oranges and apples (though it did end in war between Padua and Venice). Chivalry was a new climax of Christian feeling, and it was St Francis, the *jongleur de Dieu*, who brought it into Italy rather than any knight. In the century of his birth the Immaculate Conception was celebrated for the first time ; the Virgin took on a new significance as a figure of peace and gentleness. The woman was a revered creature in herself ; her hand was kissed by a man whenever he entered the room ; servants bore her train ; her beauty was united to her virtue in one idea, part and parcel of a certain radiance of character, expected of every noble woman. *Virtù* meant not virtue in our present rather pathetic sense but integrity, or more exactly radiant spirit.

And the *cicisbeo* was a lover in that sense. It is true that he frequently became an actual lover in the eighteenth century, but only because the tradition of chivalry was lost by that time. It became a form, as spirit itself tended to decline, through the freethinkers and encyclopedists. That was what Carlo Gozzi meant when he said that in Venice women had become men, and men women, and that both were monkeys. Gozzi was, so to speak, the last real devotee of Petrarch and Plato : little wonder he found Venice a mess.

The *cicisbeo* attended his lady at all times. He got her theatre tickets, handed her into the gondola, fetched servants for her, waited on her at her toilet in the morning, sat at her side at dinner, stayed close by her in the opera-box. If the relation was a smooth one it meant continual titillation – and petty bickering and snapping if it was not. Not even in the country were they free of each other. In Goldoni's *La Villeggiatura* it is taken for granted that you do not make love to your *cicisbeo* : he is a kind of foppish necessity ; no fashionable husband can lift up his head while his wife lacks her 'servant'. There is even a sense that sex is a little vulgar. And noble people were tired. For many titillation was the main pleasure. When the relation with the

G

cicisbeo did plunge into sex it was looked on as a momentary if understandable collapse of the system.

The women were vivacious, as well as sweet; there was a certain type of Venetian beauty which can be seen still today, captured best by Iacopo Palma in the seated woman of his *Sacred Conversation*: fair-haired with bright, large eyes, a rather bulbous nose and large gentle lips. But frivolity was now beginning to mark their expressions and therefore their faces. You could not have great beauty for long where there was no gravity, where responsibility did not weigh on people now and then. Prettiness took its place, little by little. Because foreigners were excluded from the drawing rooms sexual intrigues were discussed in front of the women with complete candour. It was like a vast family gone to incest. No one had the slightest hesitation in mentioning love, unless it was so scandalous as to place itself outside the rules of polite society.

There was one place where a lady could do what she liked without worrying about danger or decorum, and that was inside the cabin of a gondola. Any gondolier who betrayed a wife to her husband would have been drowned next day by his colleagues, though violent methods like these had become rather theoretical by the eighteenth century. The gondola was in fact replacing the convent as the place for assignations by the middle of the century. The days when a convent had the 'honour' of finding a nice mistress for the papal nuncio were nearly gone by that time.

Président de Brosses said that the nuns of Venice (meaning pupils at the convents) were to his mind the most attractive women of them all, and that if he had stayed longer he would have given them closer attention. Those he saw at Mass behind the grille, talking and laughing among themselves throughout, were pretty and dressed so as to catch the eye. They had charming caps, simple cloaks which were nearly always white, and they showed as much neck and shoulder as French actresses.

Really the convents were finishing schools for patrician girls whose education had never started. There they waited patiently for marriage, and were chosen from the other side of the enclosure grille like goldfish in a pond. In his memoirs Goldoni describes how one of the pretty pupils at the convent of S. Francesco was offered to him by an older nun whom he happened to know: in the end the girl was settled on a rich guardian, and the excuse he got was that the guardian would soon be dead, and would leave her a fortune, after which he himself could marry her.

From the point of view of the state, convents were good places for the temporary imprisonment of virgins, before they were plucked for marriage; nothing could possibly fill girls' minds while they were in them. Even the Gospel was never taught them; its subversive sincerity made the Old Testament safer ground. The convents were under the control of the *provveditori sopra monasteri*, who in fact safeguarded them as fashionable centres. The pope protested again and again; Gregory XIII said, 'I am pope everywhere except in Venice, but to no effect'.

Convents were really little salons, under an abbess who was usually a Loredano or Rezzonico or Dandolo daughter; having failed to find a husband, or sometimes through choice, she remained inside. Besides entertaining guests, pupils spent their time singing, dancing and reciting; at carnival time the *parlatorii*, or front parlours, became little theatres where their gifts were shown off, and balls were held in the refectory. Married women came to the little courts with their *cicisbei*, and the intense ogling and pretty gossip that had been left behind in the bedroom went on in the conventional parlour.

Even so, there were still nuns with a vocation, like Carlo Gozzi's sister, Clare. He badgered her for three months to leave her convent but she refused. She told him that the only way he could get her out was by cutting her into small pieces. Later on he realized that she was by far the happiest female in the family.

While the law forbade women to bring a law-suit or stand security for other people or even give evidence, they could act independently of their husbands if they argued their case well. A widow could live in her husband's house for a year and one day after his death, or as long as her dowry was not paid back. If she lived with her sons she had a right to food and clothing until they were of age. Dowries were protected. The Republic was hard on men who made false promises of marriage, or abandoned a woman after seducing her. Even in the eighteenth century this was so: when the young Steffani of Casanova's memoirs abandoned a count's daughter to whom he had promised marriage there was a hunt for him throughout the Venetian territories, during which time Casanova seduced her himself (though he was wise enough to make any promises).

Because of the Venetian policy of never enlarging a woman's mind no great patronesses came into being; there were no Medici, Orsini, Colonna women. Cassandra Fidele had been famous in fifteenth-century Venice because so rare – rather like the gigantic Magrat who astonished Venice in 1757 by being over seven feet tall and nearly forty stone in weight. The traditional Venetian woman was healthy, direct, voluptuous, and happy to be so. The much lighter creature of the eighteenth century was a result of the neo-classical mania that produced Arcadia clubs up and down the peninsula, and insipid poetry that cited the virtue of women as higher than that of men. The wife and mother became less important in this shower of Latin compliments; the refined woman more so. The absurdities of Arcadian verse were lavished on all the great Venetian beauties – Lugrezia and Maria Contarini, Elena Foscari, Cecilia Morosini, Laura Badoer, Marina Mocenigo, Paola Pisani: they were all turned into Petrarch's Laura, in verse that would have turned Petrarch's stomach. But together with the refinement came greater directness of speech, and promiscuity, and cynicism, for the simple reason that the courtesans were now the real female aristocracy: the men wanted even their women of pleasure to have been praised by the versifiers. Chivalry was now in the service of sex.

When we remember the Sumptuary Law of 1299 which fixed only four dresses for a bride's trousseau, only one girdle of pearls, only one string of gold worth more than ten *soldi*, not more than two cloaks of ermine, only one mantle lined with silk, only a cubit's length for trains, we shall realise how times had changed. Every trick had been used to avoid these rules, and in fact the surveillance became so impracticable in the fourteenth century that one law was revoked after only seven years. Later enactments said that no silver waistbands should be worth more than ten ducats; and so it went on, until by the fifteenth century, when the laws were still in force, some women were wearing pearls to the value of six hundred ducats. By the eighteenth century no extravagance was barred. Some of the dresses that remain on view today from that time are still breathtaking; sumptuous, graceful, brilliant – embroidered with marvellous care, with layer on layer of brocade, gold thread, silk and lace reaching to the feet, stiff bodices and half-sleeves with lacy frills, side-bustles and farthingales. Nothing was spared in colour, in generous cut; sometimes precious lace was elaborately sprayed over the neckpiece and the skirt as well as the sleeves; the women showed plenty of bosom, the V-necks going straight from the shoulder, the square necks set very low.

Angelo Labia the dialect-poet had something to say about this:

> *Conzier da furie, mate spiritae,*
> *Cavei sul muso sempre sparpagnai,*
> *Colo nuo afato e in colo ben spalae,*
> *E do peti mostrar sempre spacai;*
>
> *Un taglio sul bustin da relassae,*
> *Sporto in fora da drio come i tolai;*
> *Cotole e vesto curte e curte assae,*
> *E sfiamesanti veli sui cendai;*
>
> *Calza bianca e mulete e gran cordele,*
> *Puzae con languidezza sul Servente,*
> *Caminar da pitoche o Buranele . . .*

'Hair in the style of furies and mad spirits, always in disorder, all over your faces, your necks completely naked, your shoulders uncovered, showing more and more bosom! The cut of your dress is casual, you stick out at the back like tables, your skirts are short, you have flaming veils over your *zendadi*, white stockings and shawls and great ribbons, as you lean on your *cicisbeo* with a languid air, walking like waifs!'

The women painted their faces and their bosoms. They kept to the tradition of spending hours on their *altane* bleaching their hair. As girls they went out dressed in a simple veil of silk, called the *fazzuolo*,

which covered their faces and chests: but once they were married
no splendour was barred. Women's fashions had always changed
quickly in Venice, had always been sensitive to foreign influence, but
never before had they been rich at all costs. So real elegance suffered.
The fact that your body was hidden under layers of expensive brocade
and silk, with flounces, pleats, puffs, elaborate stays, hoops and bustles
– however much neck or bosom or calf you showed – meant that
you could never have real grace of line. Someone remarked that the
woman was the least part of the show. But still, the show was dazzling.
There was a mass of ribbon, lace, veil, flowered silk: even shoes were
painted with bright colours. Angelo Labia was right: it was refinement
to a point of madness, and ecstasy quite beyond elegance.

The *zendado* (usually abbreviated to *zendà*) was a long veil thrown
over the head and shoulders and then tied round the waist with a knot
at the back; towards the end of the Republic its effect was less to
veil the person than to set off the brilliant gold thread and quilted
satin underneath, the enamelled flowers and Holland (linen) cloth and
muslin and camelot (cloth of camel or goat's hair) and ermine. Even
as a veil it was embellished with lace edges. Underclothes were as
elaborate, with gold buttons and the finest silver lace embroidery.

On holidays patrician women had to wear the official black *vesta*
or silk robe with the *zendà* over it, but they cheated by letting go
on all the other articles – the bustled skirts, the low-cut necks (to give
space for jewellery) and laced sleeves. The habit of very tight stays
meant that the bosom was thrown forward and as high as physically
possible. Compared to the prevailing French fashions Venetian dress
was fanciful, frivolous, gaily inconsequential, with all kinds of indi-
vidual little touches which Parisians thought bizarre. The great doll in
the Merceria (the *Piavola de Franza*) was dressed with the latest French
fashions, but its new ideas were only taken as a stimulus to more
wildness. Venetian hats, for instance, were a climax of extravagant
attention and bad taste; they bore fruit and feathers and stuffed birds
and butterflies and masses of flowers; sometimes they looked like a
magic cabbage-patch, so enormous that you could hardly recognise the
wearer as a woman. The hair underneath was elaborate enough without

....

a hat: it was piled high, with false hair added, in pyramids and baskets and fans and towers (called *cimieri* or *conzieri*). A style called *pouf à sentiment* contained locks of hair belonging to your lover or some member of your family, and was decorated with little portraits of that person, or even of a pet, or both. Sometimes a head took a small fortune to dress, with precious stones, and flowers specially picked ; the whole was sometimes so big that it had to be held together with iron hoops. Then it was powdered, though the powder might be crawling with bugs, seen scaling a little 'tower'. Washing was never popular among the great ladies: they preferred creams and rouge. Perfume was excellent for disinfecting the person, and clothes were drenched in it – gloves, hats and stockings ; since nothing smells staler than stale perfume, clothes at least must have been washed frequently. The face, apart from its layer of pink rouge, was patched, and the position of the patch meant something quite precise: one near the eye was called *irresistibile,* one in the middle of the brow *maestosa* or 'majestic', one at the corner of the eye *passionata*, on the lip or cleft of the chin *galante*, at the corner of the mouth *assassina* or 'murderess'. Fingernails were worn very long. And jewels (not always genuine) were of course flung everywhere on the exposed parts – the face, neck, bosom, hands, wrists, a riot of necklaces, ear-rings, chains, bracelets, brooches, clasps. Fans were sometimes masterpieces of intricate work, made of parchment or silk or fine paper, with handles of ivory, silver or gold, tortoise-shell or mother of pearl, and studded with gems.

In this last epoch women exercised their greatest influence in obvious and visible things, and lost it in all the important things, such as the making of homes, and the management of family interests where they touched marriage and dowries and a career for the son. Like their husbands they were virtually strangers to their children ; at least, that was the case in the greatest families. Their influence came out in much artistic activity, and little or no art: in prettiness and clever craftsmanship, in miniatures and small gossipy pictures, in poems that touched no problem. Refinement had settled on Venetian life ; its love was without much passion ; even voluptuous desires seemed tired. The eye was enchanted everywhere : no cause for indignation, rebellion, friction of any kind; the heart was never addressed. If we look carefully at the Pietro Longhi pictures (a room in the Ca' Rezzonico is devoted to them) we shall see that lightness and coolness are everything. There is the murmur of light talk, the tinkle of cups and the rustle of bedclothes. The solemnity has gone. There are glimpses of the drawing room, the tailor's shop, the alchemist's, a lady's toilet, the dancing lesson, chocolate time soon after rising, the seller of fried doughnuts, a stroll on the Liston (now a fashionable affair more than one of rank), the embroidery shop, the country dance called *La Furlana*. The Venetians themselves seem anonymous. They look silently towards us.

From the time women took to low heels, with the approval of their men, they began to mingle in public, no longer stylised, no longer stern, distant creatures. They lived in an endless hum of talk and flattery, in the hints and shadows of love affairs when not in affairs themselves.

As always when something is rotten in the state of Denmark they seemed to like nothing better than undressing in public. The theatres were badly lit, to a thrilling extent. At the end of a performance, because there were no lights in the auditorium or the boxes, the audience had to grope its way towards the lanterns held at the exits by waiting gondoliers. Half-way through the century the Inquisitors forbade the lady who owned the theatre of S. Benedetto, a Pisani-Grimani, from standing at the entrance of her box showing too much of her bare self, as she might 'cause grave disorder'. And a year later two other young women were put under house-arrest for letting down their *baule* to below their shoulders, in the darkness of their boxes.

The women even had political influence now. Their presence was felt in the dispensing of favours, in lawsuits and political intrigues of the kind that removed Gratarol from the public scene after he had been parodied by Carlo Gozzi on the stage. But there were no politics to speak of. The politicians still existed, though with little to get their teeth into: there were intelligent men among them, fully capable of doing what their predecessors had done, but tied down by lack of effectual power, or any recognisable will in the people. Catherine

....

La zentildonna

OPPOSITE The toilet

OVERLEAF The *parlatorio*

Dolfino Tron, though a great woman socially, never had the ear of
the highest politicians of the time. And then politics bored the women.
The new ideas coming from France had no effect on them; true, by the
end of the régime great ladies were making tricolour cockades, but
only because it was the fashion. On the whole, the imminence of
Venice's downfall was unknown to the women of the city. It was un-
dreamed of. In Isabella Albrizzi's famous *conversazione* politics were
never discussed, though Ippolito Pindemonte (who later wrote a poem
in praise of the French revolution) was a frequent visitor. It was not
only lack of interest, though. Fear of the ducal palace still lingered.
The legend of the Inquisitors persisted, even if their real power did not.
That was why foreigners had to remain spectators of the licence
among the women, or rather the apparent licence: an affair between
a patrician woman and a foreigner was scotched at once; no wonder
few countries continued full ambassadorial representation in Venice
now that there was no political need – their staffs had died of boredom
in the old days.

Nowhere in Europe was a wife externally more independent of her
husband. They were seldom together now, unless one happened to pass
the other in the corridor of a casino, masked. That did not necessarily mean promiscuity, but it did mean that the serious side of love
had been played out. In 1747 the Inquisitors closed a casino on the
Giudecca belonging to Caterina Sagredo Barbarigo, and a few years
later that of Marina Sagredo Pisani on the Ponte dei Forali, though they
both moved to new addresses. Cecilia Priuli Valmarana's was shut
down after she had screamed abuse at a patrician. But closing was
simply a sign of disapproval; no more was intended.

The Inquisitors were particularly anxious to prevent the noble classes
from carrying their free habits to the ordinary people; flunkies and
concierges were now used as spies. Once a woman had offended them
they hounded her as relentlessly as they would have hounded a traitor
a century before. Madaluzza Gradenigo had a lover in Udine and gave
endless parties. When her husband died she married another Gradenigo,
the ambassador in Paris at that time, but the Inquisitors refused to
allow her to join him. When she disobeyed a later order not to join

....
Lady with a fan

her husband in Constantinople they sentenced her to three months' banishment, though it was to one of her own houses in the Este. A decree of 1774 said that a patrician lady should show an example to the rest of society; it was the first time the matter had been put so clearly. This was not really a moral concern: it showed fear of revolution, which was the one thing that brought the patrician class down in the end, if any one thing did.

Only in Venice could you see a minister of state being tapped playfully on the nose by a great courtesan at the theatre. One lovely lady used to keep a dagger in her bosom at all times; she said she used it for the management of her 'private affairs'. (Zulietta, Jean-Jacques Rousseau's lover, kept two pistols on her dressing table.) But then even nuns and abbesses carried weapons; an abbess once had a poniard duel with a nun over a mutual lover, the *abbé* de Pomponne; and the duel only made a scandal because it took place within the convent walls. People thought that if nuns were going to fight they should do it on unconsecrated ground!

Love affairs, when they happened, tended to be quick and not to leave regrets. Both parties preferred freedom to love-ties. They entered an affair for pleasure and made no bones about it; and when it ceased to give pleasure they escaped. Perhaps the most faithful lovers in Venice were the nuns. Certainly Casanova's greatest affair was with the nun he calls 'MM', who was as near to a female version of himself as a human being could get. She chose her pleasures with the same strategic skill, and did not even confine them to men. She used sex as he did – to express an ardent state of general adoration; therefore quick exchanges of lover were necessary, because sex quickly exhausted the adoration.

According to Mrs Thrale, Venetian women were too greedy of pleasure to be lovely: 'Like all sensualists . . . they fail of the end proposed, from hurry to obtain it, and consume those charms which alone can procure them continuance or change of admirers; they injure their health, too, irreparably, and that in their earliest youth, for few remain unmarried till fifteen, and at thirty have a wan and faded look. '*On ne goûte pas ses plaisirs ici, on les avale*' ('They do not taste

....

their pleasures here, they swallow them'), said Madame la Présidente yesterday very judiciously.' She found the Venetian woman needed neither restraint nor training, she was naturally of such a sweet manner that she was admired without effort on her part ; 'she really charms without any settled intent to do so, merely from that irresistible good-humour and mellifluous tone of voice which seize the soul and detain it in despite of Juno-like majesty or Minerva-like wit.'

Not everyone testifies that they were Junoesque, though. Mrs Thrale may have thought so, being small herself. An Englishman called Howel, a contemporary of hers, thought them small ; the tall hair-do accounted for the appearance of height sometimes. As to dress, Mrs Thrale said that the Venetian woman had 'no room to show taste in dress or invent new fancies and disposition of ornaments for tomorrow. The Government takes all that trouble off her hands, knows every pin she wears, and where to find her at any moment of the day or night.' This only shows how successfully the splendour was hidden under the *zendà*, the *baula*, the black silk *vesta*. All Mrs Thrale noticed was the *zendà*, 'a full black petticoat of silk, training a very little on the ground ; then on the head was a skeleton wire, over which was loosely thrown this hood of black mode or persian, so as to shade the face like a cur-tain ; the thin silk that remains to be disposed of they roll back so as to discover the bosom, fasten it with a puff before at the top of their stomacher, and, once more rolling it back from the hip, tie it gracefully behind, and let it hang in two long ends.' That was morning wear ; but the evening brought Mrs Thrale no closer glimpse of what lay underneath : 'The evening ornament is a rather masculine silk hat, with sometimes one feather ; a great black silk cloak lined with white, with a vast, heavy round handkerchief of black lace, which lies over neck and shoulders, and conceals shape and all completely. Here is surely little appearance of art, no craping or frizzing the hair, which is flat on the top and all of one length, hanging in long curls about the back or sides as it happens. No brown powder, and no rouge at all. Thus without variety does a Venetian lady contrive to delight the eye, and without much instruction, too, to charm the ear.' Yet she did see them sometimes, in boats, 'their beauties unveiled upon the water' ;

she was deceived by so much outward observance of the Sumptuary Laws on official occasions, as she was meant to be.

Once, people had thought Venetian women stiff. A century before, Charles Emanuel of Savoy had tried to kiss a Contarini's arm, and had got this reply: 'If these are the manners of Turin, they are quite unknown here, and your Highness will never succeed in bringing them, either.' She could not have been more wrong. The pride softened with the virtue: the woman of the eighteenth century is livelier and sweeter, more sensitive ; the health and fullness of the flesh – those bright, regular teeth and large lips and firm figures – were touched with something misty now, a dreamy glow. The worship of women always produces beauty in them, and so sweetness radiated through Venetian faces, doing twice the work of flesh and bone.

In 1709 Frederick IV of Denmark asked Rosalba to do portraits of the twelve most beautiful women in the city: only eight of these still exist – the ladies Mocenigo, Pisani, Zenobio, Cornaro, Correr, Foscari, Labia and Barbarigo. Everything in their faces, shoulders and bosoms suggests ease ; they seem to be hearing about love all day, lazing between one light sensation and another.

In a way, perhaps, the *cicisbeo* (himself usually a husband) was the husband's hired man, to feed his wife on praise. A husband could clearly not do it himself. It was all, in the end, a shade perverted ; and, as Mrs Thrale says, it ate up the nerves and even beauty in the end. Perhaps the most satisfied couples were those who hated each other and agreed to take a secondary husband and wife, to whom they were then faithful ; it was perhaps the most temperate answer of them all.

Yet love-affairs could even now achieve remarkable power. Marina Benzon wrote to her lover, the Marchese Rangoni, 'Poor Marina, who can only offer her Beppo a heart ardent with love and desire to make him happy ! Oh, believe me, I would like to prove my immense love for you with some great sacrifice ! . . . Seducer, what have you done to me ?'

A great part of the day was naturally passed in front of a mirror, for a great woman. She was never alone. The hairdresser (sometimes her lover and confidant, since access to her bedroom was easier for him than for even the *cicisbeo*) came to her after she had finished her morning chocolate. Her *cicisbeo* and perhaps other friends helped her lace her bosom, with compliments. In the afternoon there was dinner (for which much toilet preparation was necessary), followed by more mirror-sitting. Later they all went out or sang or played instruments, or simply gossiped. It is easy to see that radiant happiness was not all the story. It was a narrow, treadmill life which many, like Casanova and some of the young noblemen who took frequent journeys to London and Paris, were happy to leave.

Some slightly nervous, fluttering quality shows through their portraits (usually painted when they were in full bloom). Of course they were hypochondriacs. Like their contemporaries in the rest of Europe they tended to faint at bad news, and were suffocated by tight stays and vast bustles. But it was not all tight stays either: French, not to say English, sentimentality was oozing across Europe; everyone in Venice read Jean-Jacques Rousseau and Richardson (and Goldoni's dramatisation of *Pamela* helped). Women identified themselves with heroines like Pamela, who to our eyes is a bit of a humbug. They tried to curb their natural health for the sake of a sick frailty; this was beginning to be thought – perhaps as a long-term effect of neo-classicism, of platonism gone rotten – proper to the female sex.

One of the most famous beauties of the early eighteenth century was Lucrezia Basadonna, the wife of the Procurator Mocenigo. We see her sitting before us in a Rosalba portrait looking bright, erect, black-eyed, full of an alert and trusting curiosity, with the famous Mocenigo pearls round her neck (hence her name 'Mocenigo of the pearls'). She fell in love with an Englishman, who scandalized her admirers by being unfaithful to her; no Venetian would have been that philistine.

But Venice's woman of really classic fame, towards the end of the eighteenth century, was Catarina Dolfin, married first to a Tiepolo and then, after the annulment of the marriage, to Andea Tron, already an old man. When she married the second time at thirty-six years of age Tron's immense riches seemed like Venice's official tribute to her:

she would certainly inherit them quickly. She wrote to him, 'All over !' (meaning her youth and fame, now that they were getting married); *'lisciata, pettinata e colla mia lingua mi impegno di vincer tutte le giovani'* ('painted, combed and with my wit I undertake to beat all the young ones !'). She had blue eyes, smooth golden hair, and was so famous for her beauty that her husband lost a strong chance of becoming doge ; she was respected and listened to in the highest quarters, but not liked. Like an increasing number of great women at this time she gave her opinions on public affairs in her brilliant salons. And she was at the centre of Carlo Gozzi's parody of Gratarol, who was guilty, some said, of never having found her beautiful (in fact he had gone further and called her a whore and political wire-puller). She was said to be behind many of her government's decrees. She was astute, and no snob. Once she wrote to the Duke of Gian Galeazzo Serbelloni, when he was occupied with younger mistresses, 'All I ask is that a gentleman should treat me like a gentleman.'

Carlo Gozzi's play *Le Drohge d'Amore* clearly had no strong satirical intentions behind it ; in any case it was an adaptation of a Spanish work, like a number of others he had done after his fables had began to pall. But Venice began talking about it as a caricature of Gratarol before the curtain went up. Gratarol was a secretary of the Senate and had just been appointed ambassador in Naples. He was an outlandish man to look at ; he had powerful enemies. He walked in what was called 'the English manner', a round, swaying step. But the play would have ended as it had begun, as a bore, hated even by its author, had it not been for the two women involved, one the *prima donna* of the stage company and the other La Tron. The *prima donna*, Teodora Ricci, had lost Gozzi as her *cicisbeo* (perhaps lover) because she had allowed very public visits from Gratarol : and almost certainly she began to spread it about that the play was a jealous revenge on Gozzi's part. As for La Tron, the script came to her from Sacchi, the actor-manager of the troupe, after murmurs about its being a parody had started, and before it was produced. La Tron had once been Gratarol's friend ; she was now his enemy. And Gratarol seems to have lost his head. He took the gossip seriously and tried to get the production

....

stopped, which only spurred his enemies on and secured a full house
for the first night ; it also meant that the actors, unknown to Gozzi,
dressed the play as a parody. When Don Adone, a small part, walked
on he was Gratarol to the T. After the opening performance Gratarol
was ridiculed wherever he went, or at least pointed out. This was the
sort of scandal that rocked modern Venice.

Gratarol induced the *prima donna* to indispose herself for one performance. He wrote Gozzi a letter of abuse. Gozzi took this letter
to La Tron, an act which brought Gratarol down in a few days.
For it was she who kept the play on the stage when the author wanted
it withdrawn, and who forced Gratarol through an agent of the Ten
to write a sweet letter of apology to Gozzi (though verbally he
promised to kiss his arse) ; it was she who by influence deprived him of
his ambassadorship at Naples and sent him raging out of the country.
The Ten even made a performance of the play obligatory by public
decree, and had the *prima donna* accompanied to the theatre by one
of their guards. There was no limit to the pettiness on all sides, including Gozzi's ; his philosophy of quiet forbearance was ruffled by the
insults.

No one suggested or even thought of a duel. But then all of Venice's
rages these days had a harmless theatrical tone. In any other epoch
Gozzi would certainly have called Gratarol out, or vice versa. But all
he did was prowl round the S. Moisè casino waiting for the other man
in the dark, and then go home feeling rather rash and heroic about
having done so. Gratarol made sure not to leave his house : he was a
healthy, energetic man (not qualities to get him friends in Venice),
but felt happier handing round *diavoloni* (delicious Neapolitan sweets
filled with liqueur) than duelling.

La Tron's sister-in-law, Cecilia Zeno Tron, was nearly as famous,
and perhaps a kinder woman. She was a slim creature and so spirited
and cheerful that she immunised herself against old age (though she
did spend a fortune on cosmetics). When she let her box at the
S. Benedetto theatre for a gala evening someone made up a verse about
her having sold the seats for a higher price than she was prepared to
'let' even her own person : to which she replied, '*Gavè razon, perchè*

questa, al caso, la dono' – 'you're quite right, because sometimes I give the latter away for nothing !'

Perhaps the nicest and loosest woman was Marina Querini Benzon, or '*la Benzona*' as she was called, the daughter of Pietro Antonio Querini. She was also called '*la Biondina*', and had a long arched nose, delicately reflective lips, and eyes that have been described as passionately alert, like a bird's. Longhi's picture of her conveys a special thrill in her person, sparkling and yet collected, tranquil. Her smallness suggested pluck, something daredevil ; yet there was always gentleness underneath. Her lovers were like that too – one after the other.

She was quite different, except in the Venetian quality of her nose, from Contarina Barbarigo with her piled hair and clear, large, intelligent face ; Contarina was such a clever talker that Joseph II is said to have remained on his feet for five hours in conversation with her at a ball (though some witnesses give him at least a chair). And she introduced Byron to La Guiccioli. She had the best, the only real wit of all, direct and unmalicious ; her presence was apparently so delightful that Joseph spoke about her for months afterwards in Vienna. Wit ran in her gifted family. Caterina Dolfin, dedicating some sonnets to Contarina's mother in 1767, described the Barbarigo virtues on the distaff side as 'humanity, courtesy, prudence, greatness without pride, womanliness with education and virtue'. On the other hand this same Barbariga had one of the liveliest casinos in Venice, so lively that the Inquisitors closed it down.

Venice had no blue-stockings. The *conversazioni* centred not on talk, or on ideas, but on the women. Almost everything said was directed to them, from one or more *cicisbeo*. Literary men came, but they were as gossipy as the rest. Président de Brosses described the *conversazione* at the Foscarini house as a bore : all he got was a slice of water-melon at eleven in the evening, followed by a cup of coffee, and almost no conversation.

The great *conversazioni* were those of the Pisani, the Rezzonici, the Tron families ; they were less exclusive than ever before, and even foreigners were invited, though this was still against the law. Chocolate and coffee were served. They were never noisy : the conversation was easy, unguarded, intimate. It was not confined to the drawing room but went on at the casino, at the theatre, and back at the house afterwards, until the middle of the night. Sometimes the talk was splendid, and was remembered like a song for long afterwards.

Caterina Dolfin Tron held her salon every Monday evening at the S. Giuliano casino: it was perhaps through minds like hers that French ideas began to enter the Republic. These were not thought disturbing, even when they were expressly revolutionary: they were simply new – one more facet of the game. Also they combined easily with the atmosphere of the salon because they were witty and cutting; above all, they were cynical at bottom like Venetian society, and when not any of these things they were conveniently sentimental. To sport the new ideas was rather like sporting a new style of hat. It meant that patricians nowadays preferred being in the fashion to being either powerful or safe: they therefore failed to recognise the seriousness of the new thought; they failed to see its sincerely anti-aristocratic side.

French ideas became such a fashion in Caterina Dolfin Tron's circle, which included both the Gozzi brothers, Angelo Querini and Giorgio Pisani (two of Venice's most famous radicals), that the Inquisitors decided to close the S. Giuliano casino down.

The most respectable salon belonged to Donna Isabella, the Princess Rasini from Rome: the most powerful Venetians went there, and it was even safe for the doge to be seen drinking her chocolate. The gayest and least consequential salons, sporting neither power nor radicalism, were those of Cecilia Zeno Tron and Marina Querini Benzon: even the fall of the Republic hardly disturbed *their* pleasant talk.

Chapter 9

'Liberty and Licence'

Love – or rather, love-making – was the theme of their books, their snuff-boxes, their rings and visiting cards, and it often toppled into the obscene. Verses were illustrated with erotic woodcuts. The reading matter was either romance or gallantry. The old ideal of cutting a fine figure now meant cutting more or less a sexual one: even the men studied themselves in the mirror for hours, rehearsing poses and gestures and ways of taking or offering snuff. The *cicisbeo* rustled and tinkled as he walked along at his mistress's side, loaded with ornament, powdered and laced. Quite often he had less than no appeal for her – he was an accepted formality, laid down in the marriage contract; his 'muscles of cotton wool', as Carlo Gozzi described them, were only required for carrying eyeglasses and cups of chocolate and snuff boxes.

What the freedom of women in the eighteenth century did was to dethrone the courtesan, who now tended to become a common whore; it also abolished the necessity of convents as places of assignation and wife-choosing. The sexual market was thrown open. Respectable women even became available to the foreigner. There was a famous love-affair between the French ambassador Froullay and a nun of noble birth called Maria da Riva. It was so ardent that it attracted the notice of the Inquisitors, who ordered Maria not to appear in the convent's *parlatorio* when the ambassador called. Froullay took this as a personal insult, complained to the government and went on seeing her. This time the Inquisitors had her moved to Ferrara; the result was that she fell in love with somebody else, and married him. Not even an ambassador could complain about that.

On the other hand, the government was lenient to prostitutes: no more than any other government in Italy did it try to suppress them. The Venetian father (like the Italian father until very recently) encouraged his son to buy his sex, on his social level. If he combined high social position with small funds he clubbed together with his friends to share a courtesan. Shared love in Venice was never quite the sin it was in the rest of Christendom. Casanova tells us that he shared a young married woman with five or six friends, and that they made love to her one after the other, and that her cheeks were flushed with joy. The two sisters Casanova deprived of their virginity (losing his own as well) never quarrelled over him; they were repentant because they slept with him but not because they shared him.

A middle-class woman once put up her daughter's honour in a lottery, and sold tickets at a sequin a piece. Some of the noblemen are said to have sold their wives in a subtler way. La Tron rightly said when she was introducing the Princess Gonzaga (a woman of loose reputation) in Venetian society, 'She belongs to an illustrious family. As for the rest I will not answer for her – nor for you, nor for myself!'. Carlo Gozzi's conclusion was that most women were barely capable of love: what men mistook for love was simply vanity or ambition – they wanted to ensnare people, and the more powerful their victims the better they liked it. Or else they cast out their nets for a husband, using the same social calculations. But then he did not blame them. He maintained that the men had started it all, by pouring compliments into their ears night and day, and encouraging their little weaknesses. His work in the theatre proved for him that Venetian women were disloyal precisely to the degree their men were, and not more so.

'There is no place in the world where liberty and licence reign more entirely,' Président de Brosses said. 'Don't meddle in politics and you can do what you like. The Venetian temper is so sweet that, despite the warm blood and the liberty given by masks, the allurements of the night, the narrow lanes, above all the bridges without parapets from which men could be pushed into the sea without anyone noticing, there are hardly more than four accidents of this kind a year, and that only among visitors.'

The fact was that the men were determined – much more than the women – to burn out the last powers of the Republic as quickly as possible, and enfeeble themselves to a point where they could no longer govern their own houses, let alone the state. Servants nowadays were disobedient, familiar; the women complained that when they ordered chocolate for their friends they got either nothing at all or stale coffee. Servants had always been one of the family; it was the family that was now going to seed.

The rich had one remaining standard of honour, one source of rivalry – personal ostentation. The famous story that Labia threw all his gold plate out of the window into the Grand Canal after a banquet is believed by almost no one, yet it is probably true: perhaps he did it to show off, or just to make the pun on his own name, '*L'abbia o no l'abbia, sono sempre Labia*' ('whether I have it or not I am still Labia'). And the sequel story – that he had his servants stationed below to catch it – is as probable as the first.

In his memoirs Longo describes how he took fifty-three friends to his villa on the Brenta by two boats, one of which had eighteen musicians dressed as Arabs, the other twenty-four servants dressed as Quakers. At night they embarked again meaning to return to Venice, but on their way past the Corner villa they noticed that it was brilliant with chandeliers and torches, and that an orchestra was playing inside; a kind of serenade started, between the house orchestra and the floating one; he and his guests were asked inside, and they danced all night, and stayed to dinner next day, all fifty-three of them, with their servants taken care of below stairs. The hors d'oeuvre and the dessert were designed like miniature Arabs and Quakers, in imitation of Longo's own party. The host happened to tell his major-domo to return some unwanted roasted pheasants to the kitchen for the next day. The main guest, Marco Gradenigo, said he thought this was a stingey thing to do. Not that he really thought so: it was a challenge, the eighteenth-century equivalent of a medieval joust. Corner, playing his part, said that since Gradenigo never offered so much as a glass of water to his guests (Gradenigo was one of the most lavish entertainers in Venice) he had no right to complain. A typical competition started. Each house gave a banquet on alternate days, struggling to provide bigger and better dishes. It went on for ten days. That was heroism in modern Venice.

As to what these men did in their free time – free, that is, of banquets and balls and love-making – is not at all an open question: they dabbled. And since their gifts were as lavish as their tables they could do it successfully. Longo himself was a lawyer, a horse-doctor (as a joke), a private tutor, a theatrical impresario, an improviser of verse.

Nearly all these men died, so to speak, with the Republic. Hardly one of the really gifted ones had a placid death. Casanova died mocked by servants (they kept his portrait in the lavatory). Gasparo Gozzi tried to commit suicide by throwing himself into the Brenta. Rosalba died blind. In Paris Goldoni was only just spared by the Terror, and died destitute. Tiepolo was in misery. Vivaldi died in Vienna, poor and forgotten. Sacchi, Venice's finest actor-manager, died penniless at sea.

Outwardly the nobles were still a recognisable class; from the visitor's point of view (though not from their own) they had centuries more of power to exercise. They still wore their distinctive costume of black silk to their knees, with breeches of printed calico, and a large black, sometimes red or violet, toga (wool for the winter, silk for the summer). The senators wore an ell of cloth on their left shoulder, to correspond with the colour of their toga. They had vast wigs, though in the eighteenth century there were prominent enemies of the wig, the most famous of them a certain Soranzo, who liked his hair his own; the massive wig of the first half of the century gave way to the short peruke of the second half. They carried a biretta of black cloth like a night-cap. The sleeve was still of great social importance; the longer and more spacious it was, the more important the personage, until you reached the doge himself, whose sleeve reached to the ground and was made of cloth of gold.

Five years of imprisonment was the punishment for wearing the wrong toga, or for wearing none at all, but the latter part of this order was ineffectual – the official cloak tended to be used only for functions in the ducal palace. The usual dress was now a cutaway coat, breeches, silk stockings and shoes with buckles on them; that was the prevailing male fashion throughout Italy and France, but in Venice a light cloak was added. This *velada* was made of satin, cloth or velvet, and was always embroidered, laced or fringed.

The tendency since the sixteenth century was for male clothes to become more and more elaborate in cut and colour and fabric. In the seventeenth century an Italian visitor had asked if the young men of Venice wanted to change their sex, they were so gaudily dressed with tassles, bows and frills. Extravagant clothes had been a mark of wealth, but they became less and less so as the poor nobles and the not so poor merchants competed in velvets, silks, Mechlin laces, gold braid, rings and small, light shoes.

At the end of the seventeenth century silk embroidered waistcoats and doublets had come in, with gold or silver buckles for the shoes, and lace ruffles at the wrists and neck. Hair was covered with pomatum and oil of jasmine, with powder and perfume. Already in the seventeenth century young men had had rouge pots on their tables, as well as curling tongs, elegant perfume bottles and all varieties of scissors and silver-backed combs, pins and hand-mirrors. When the French periwig first hit Venice in 1665 it failed to dissuade the men from their own hair, and it was actually forbidden by the government three years later. No one took any notice of the decree and gradually it took hold. One young man was disinherited by his father for wearing a vast wig and red socks; but the youth challenged the will and got away with it by paying six thousand ducats to a charity. There were all kinds of periwig – a tall one, its tail in a black bag, called *alla dolfina*, the long-curled *groppo* and one parted in the middle called *alla cortesana*. At the beginning of the eighteenth century even the doge wore one. As a necessary result, hats tended to be carried. Trousers began to come in, replacing the Spanish breeches buckled at the knee. Here Venetians were earlier than the French, and the latter took the fashion from them. By the end of the eighteenth century dress was as casual as it had once been elaborate: it was looseness, to the point of looking *distrait*, with bare arms and bare necks for the women, no stiff bustles but the neo-classical high waist and long flowing, pleated gown, and trousers, loose jackets, casual cravats and tall floppy hats for the men. Those were the clothes of revolution.

The walks on the Liston were the same, though degenerating into what they are today – friendly strolls at aperitif time. The *Listòn de Piazza* (sometimes called *lo stradone* or 'the big road' by Venetians) was still a highly exclusive strip or 'list' of best pavement in the Piazza running by the side of the *Procuratie Vecchie*. The *Broglio* or *Brogio* was a similar strip in the Piazzetta, running from the two squat columns at the Basilica side-entrance towards the sea and alongside the ducal palace ; here the nobility walked with a more special purpose – to *brogliare pubblicamente*, that is to obtain or appeal for the lucrative jobs and honorary posts which were always in the process of changing hands. When the young nobles put on their toga for the first time, usually at the age of twenty-five, they would pass the *Broglio* several times until they were told by one of the older nobles, '*Entrar in Brogio*' or '*Vegnir in Brogio*', meaning to come inside and walk and begin their application for a privilege. Nowadays the Venetians still say, '*Andiamo fare el Listòn*' ('Let's go and do the Liston'), meaning to stroll from the entrance of the Basilica down the Piazzetta towards the sea ; thus the actual Liston has moved into the old place of the Broglio, at right angles to the original one. That is an historical development too : while the Liston became a social stroll, less and less exclusively noble as the eighteenth century wore on, the Broglio dwindled into a kind of bargaining area, rather like the *gallerie* where Italian men gather in every town and village of the peninsula today. Political or treasonable 'embroilments' were no longer possible there, as they had once been.

The education of the nobleman lost its earlier discipline. Until the seventeenth century he had to be not only a sailor but a statesman, not to say a leader. Before entering the Great Council he had to complete his two years service in the navy. He was expected to travel (at his own expense). Now he was a stay-at-home : no place in the world could offer him the ease and the pleasures of Venice. His periods in the army or navy, if any, were usually continuations of the life he had led at home, except that his women were now Dalmatian or Greek. There were few noblemen of the old stamp ; men like Francesco Pesaro and Francesco Foscari had been patrons in the grand style ; they had even been well-educated. Foscari had had thirty-eight volumes of the *Thesaurus Antiquitatum Sacrarum* printed at his own expense. But nowadays a gentle and inoffensive philistinian governed the patrician class, though it went with such benevolence and inherited good taste that it was hardly noticed. They still had eagle noses and the pout of authority, and the benign magnanimity that comes from the exercise of great power. You could read the past in their faces. But their children were now brought up by the servants; endless banquets and visits to the theatre and the *ridotto* left no time for serious fatherhood. Not that family discipline seemed to be relaxed outwardly. A child still had to kiss his parents' hands when taken downstairs, and he still must not sit down without their permission. But the taste for theatricality in everything was developed early: outdoors the child was dressed in the most luxurious clothes, silver- and gold-braided, but at home he could be as untidy as he liked, among the adoring servants. The *ballerino* taught deportment, how to kiss a hand, to dance and bow and smile, how to hold a hat with one's hand balanced on one's hip, how to hand a lady out of her chair. The more successful you were at the theatre of life the more you convinced the people round you. Casanova could get whatever he wanted because he was a born actor: only his horror at remaining stationary for any length of time prevented him from having a brilliant career in any Italian state he chose.

Almost none of the patricians went to the university of Padua now; few augmented their education by travel; few even attached themselves to the embassies abroad (at one time this had been thought a necessary schooling for work in the Great Council or Senate). The greedy passion for gambling ate away all curiosity, ambition, finally energy. What was spent created a debt for descendants. The whole class was living on the future in this way; it only needed the slightest stroke, such as Napoleon's sudden foreclosure of the conventual mortgages, for the nobility to collapse overnight.

To their most loyal servants patricians left little or nothing in their wills, mostly on the grounds that common people did not feel or need like themselves. But because they never beat their servants and

....

Masquerade
OPPOSITE Masquers on the Liston
OVERLEAF The Ridotto

allowed them their say, they were respected far more than even they usually thought, until the very end of the Republic. The more recklessly the patrician lavished money, even what was a debt to his children, the more admiration he caused ; if he showed less than a careless condescension to the people under him, they took it for self-doubt. He tried to keep his 'figure' to the last, though there was nothing for him to do but make love and dress and gamble. Greatness was expected of him, and he showed it at the expense of the state. Gambling took the place of the political and colonial adventures there had been before : it was a last rarified exercise in power and risk. In the opening lines of *La Villeggiatura* Donna Florida says to Don Eustachio, '*Vengono in villa per divertirsi, e stanno lì a struggersi ad un tavolino*' ('They come to the country to enjoy themselves, and spend all their time destroying themselves at the card table'). In this play the husband of the house refuses to give up his obsessive hunting, which gets him out of bed before dawn, while his wife refuses to give up her cards, which gets her to bed just when he is getting up. 'Why can't you stay in bed with me ?' she asks. 'What,' he says, 'twelve hours in bed ?' 'But I can't get up early !' – and there she could be speaking for a whole class.

In country or in town, the same routines of pleasure were followed. There were the same endless compliments from the *cicisbei*, the same toilet, chocolate drinking, dinner parties, balls. Venice's first season of *villeggiatura* started on 12 June with a holiday, and ended at the end of July : that was the summer one. The autumn one was from 4 October until the middle or end of November. In the first it was the great heat that drove people away from the city ; in the second the autumnal storms. The nobility travelled to their estates in little barges or *burchielli* (described by de Brosses as 'little editions of the Bucentoro'), prettily done up, with an anti-chamber for servants. Casanova described them as 'travelling houses' : all they lacked, from his point of view, was a double bed. They made slow, tranquil, pleasantly tedious journeys down the Brenta canal, drawn by horses. People climbed on the roof and sang.

The country villas lay as conveniently close to water (that of the

....
Clowns

Brenta now) as money could buy. The best of them had a Venetian splendour, with superbly laid-out gardens (not that the guests were often in the garden). The Contarini palace at Piazzòla had eighty rooms, apart from its halls and galleries, a church of its own with five organs, two theatres, a concert hall and even a printing press. Marco Contarini of the seventeenth century was largely responsible for this extravagance: in the conservatory of music which he ran there thirty-eight young girls were taught their scales (neighbours said he taught them a lot of other things too).

The Pisani villa at Strà, designed by one of Alessandro Scarlatti's librettists, Conte Gerolamo Roberti (Tiepolo did the ballroom ceiling), was perhaps the most deliberately and austerely imposing of them all. It lies at the end of a vast garden with decorative strips of water, and has six great columns at the centre of its façade. On the whole the gardens were fussy and artificial, with fountains and still pools under writhing statues, sea-horses and tritons, and gravel paths that never strayed into the dark or unexpected or natural, and hedges cut to form all kinds of recognisable shapes in case they should appear what they really were, and grass so shaved as to feel like a carpet. Napoleon chose Strà as his headquarters, hence its other name, 'La Villa Imperiale'.

In these houses, with their lavish ceilings, their vast staircases to allow access to hundreds of guests, their brilliant chandeliers and ballrooms, you recognise at once the fear of being bored. In the eighteenth century the interiors were more splendid than the exteriors; they burst on you after a simple Palladian façade. At one time the patrician had gone to his estate for exercise and farming and good air. But now he hardly went out unless to hunt or ride in his carriage. The wheat and wine harvests went on unseen. Even the hunting was decadent. At one time noblemen had hunted in parties in the Dalmatian mountains. Now they preferred decoying birds and catching them in nets. Not that they became languorous even in the country. The *villeggiatura* was a gay romp. Practical jokes soon found out the slower-minded guests: in Goldini's *La Villeggiatura* the greedy Don Ciccio (*la ciccia* is a baby-word for meat) is tied to a chair while asleep, then attacked by mock-swordsmen. You could find a dead rat in your bed at night. Salt might be offered you in place of sugar. One guest who swore he did not believe in ghosts found himself and his sheets being lifted out of the bed at night, and crayfish were released into his room with lighted candles tied to their backs.

The peasants were visited, as part of a pastoral affectation. Patrician ladies would milk cows and dance, or listen to the peasants telling stories. They would dress as shepherdesses. But gambling won. The betting tables were busy all day. Food was served more or less at all times, and the guests were free to come and go as they liked. There were three dining rooms, one for the soup and the beef, another for roasts and vegetables, a third for pudding and dessert. Almost every country house had its opera house where the best *virtuosi* sang before audiences of princes and ambassadors, sometimes numbering a thousand or more. The great hall of the house was turned into a theatre, with a proscenium arch and curtain and boxes. Liveries were extravagant, with plumes and streamers; so were the gildings and carvings on the carriages, the velvet and damask linings. Horses were magnificently buckled and reined, and it was quite usual for a carriage to be drawn by four pair. The patricians were generous to the peasants in their own way – they threw them money as they clattered past. The peasants on the mainland were perhaps Venice's most loyal subjects, even after Napoleon had occupied their lands.

Venetian merchants spent fortunes imitating all this. They reckoned *la villeggiatura* as the most expensive item of the year, and some spent more in a few rustic weeks, entertaining armies of guests, than the whole year round in Venice. Shopkeepers played the lord in front of the peasants, then returned to Venice to serve pork or bread. They got up in the afternoon, gambled, went for uncomfortable dashes in their carriages, all for the pleasure of imitation.

The noble class was shrinking. The rule that only one male in a family should marry (so as to avoid the division of family fortunes among various heirs) was having its effect: the proportion of unmarried nobles went up from about half in the sixteenth century to over sixty-six per cent in the eighteenth, and this in a class already seriously depleted by the great plagues of 1575 and 1630. By the end of the century there were not even enough noblemen to fill the necessary offices. The Golden Book had been closed at the beginning of the century, to freeze the class in its then form; and it was only opened again towards the end in an attempt to make money for the state.

There was an increasing ignorance of the foreign world among officials of state. In a letter to his cousin dated 1748 Andrea Querini said that senators these days seemed not to know what impression their policies were making on opinion abroad. They had the smallest interest in what went on in Europe, unless it was connected with fashion. In the course of its thousand years the senate had accumulated a vast knowledge of the other courts of Europe. That was all for the museum now.

But everybody still believed in Venice's political system – even the radicals did; Angelo Querini, Giorgio Pisani and Carlo Contarini, with the enthusiastic support of men like Alvise Zeno, never advocated the abolition of the constitution: nothing like a *coup d'état* was suggested in their mid-century movement. The Great Council was for them the seat of executive power, and had to be protected as such. Their doctrines were legalistic. What passed for a revolution at the end of the century, under Zorzi the shopkeeper, was rigged by the French. The nobles had long before this rendered themselves indistinguishable from the ordinary people by their own behaviour. They had long been going from one *ridotto* to another every night, taking a boat down the Brenta to their mainland villas for an early breakfast and then clattering back to Venice with a great theatrical fuss to arrive in time for the Great Council at midday (even if they did not attend it). Oriental languor settled more and more on the city; all Venice *gondolava* – leaned back on its cushions and floated through the water. Its hashish was coffee.

As for the *cicisbei*, their function of rendering a woman more and more frivolous meant the rot of society. Goldoni in his *La Dama Prudente* shows a man in love with his young wife, haunted with jealousy towards the *cicisbei* he himself has ordered her to be with all day and half the night. As Carlo Gozzi said, men were afraid of being called prejudiced. That word was thrown at almost any kind of idea that asked for discipline. Like all people who think pleasure the object of life the Venetians could see no real argument against crime, however little they were inclined to commit it. If you say that your taking pleasure in something justifies it, another man may say that the pleasure he has in killing you justifies it. The eighteenth century in Venice was the era of petty crime and corruption ; the grand days of treason were over, with their slow processions of masked men leaving the little church of S. Fantìn to the tap of drums and the slow tolling of the Campanile after the traitor's last Mass and confession. The only really respected idea was freedom from restraint. Hardly a century before, being a wife had been equivalent to holding a state position ; it had carried austere responsibilities ; now the past was thrown over as a rigid, hard-faced fashion, and everything with a taste of discipline in it fell away – probity, disinterested behaviour, language, patronage ; scraping for your own interests took their place. And you had to scrape to keep alive.

Casanova said that a certain patrician Dolfin could never get forward in Venice because he had all the old virtues. He simply could not make himself small enough to fit the new dimensions. To get on in Venice you must not awaken people's envy, their fear of rivalry, their horror of anyone shining. If you wanted 'to avoid persecution', Casanova said, you had to be like everyone else or worse. If a man had ambitions he should seem to scorn them, if handsome he had to look slovenly. It was *de rigueur* to ridicule and exclude anything foreign. A man must bow awkwardly, conceal any good taste he might have. This was what sent not only the gifted but the adventurers abroad. The field was even too narrow for adventure.

But what made eighteenth-century Venice not at all a backwater was the stupendous assortment of its gifts, nurtured through generations of power and now set free – with nowhere to go. Partly the adventurers left because Venice was a population of adventurers. It was in Paris, Vienna, that Casanova really shone. The Venetian stage was no longer big enough to play on.

Like Casanova, Lorenzo da Ponte found the Church the safest

stable for adventures, at least in youth: he was a converted Jew and wrote revolutionary verse; after the *Magistrato delle Bestemmie* accused him of eating ham on Friday he became Joseph II's playwright, wrote some of Mozart's librettos, married an Englishwoman, went broke in London as an impresario, set up as a book-seller and lastly emigrated to America, where he became a grocer and taught Italian.

Noblemen were less formal with each other than ever before. They even became friends. In the grand old days they had met each other with the superb gesture of taking off their caps with their left hand, while their right went to their hearts; they had spoken the sweetest words, open, frank, affectionate, to foreigners as well as to Venetians, but that was where it had ended. No secrets had been given away or even touched on in the frankest talk; after all, jobs had had to be fought for – magistratures, secretaryships, embassies – and they were attained more easily with a closed heart. Nowadays the whole class was living on a sinecure, and those who failed to get a decent share, the 'Barnabotti', began to form a socially unsettling class of their own.

They were often men who had ruined themselves serving the state, and eked out an existence on small state pensions. If they were very poor their children were educated free at a College of Nobles on the Giudecca, and they usually got their houses in the San Barnaba district rent-free (hence their name, 'Barnabotti'). This was perhaps the most disastrous effect of the policy of luxury begun in the sixteenth century – the creation of a large, disgruntled and above all functionless class. A second effect was the alteration of the whole concept of nobility. It quickly became what we think of it now – a matter of blood and coats of arms, in a social vacuum of vague envy and respect. Before, the Venetian nobility had been anything but a heraldic group: they had been the government, the actual Republic, in their persons; it was they who had discharged the major offices, led the navies, administered the moneys. Now, because luxury had become the chief sign by which a nobleman was recognised, brains and aptitude and energy began to count for nothing: the type of young man entering high office was an inferior one; he had been brought up to believe that money buys everything; the result was that he farmed out his work to the Secretaries for a small salary, and they, like land stewards on the mainland, consumed more and more of the benefices and perquisites. That was what produced a rotten state and a noble class of *flaneurs*.

Many families had become extinct as a result of the poor dowries to be had nowadays, and of the consequent drift of patrician women into other classes by marriage. Where a large family had been looked on as a great asset even in the previous century, it was now a disaster, because it divided up the patrimony.

Meetings of the Great Council and even the Senate were no longer regularly full: the nobles were idle and dissipated; there was hardly a senator who did not need a good night's rest. Health and a clear mind were out of fashion, as in all periods of decline. The *Savi* of the Great Council tended to take over its business, in the absence of members. In the last years of the Republic there was no real government at all; which showed how smoothly the Venetian system functioned, how automatic it was by now. Corruption in high places, hitherto unheard of, brought Venice more in line with the rest of Italy. Positions in the doge's official household were sold. Goldoni tells us that an entire state forest was cut down without governmental authority; the money trickled into the pockets of over two hundred people. As the government stood to look ridiculous, the affair was hushed up.

Spying went on, resolute and intimate as before, but without any more sense than a surviving habit: Venice was notoriously reluctant to give up anything. It descended to the trivial level; much of it was theatre censorship, and the reporting of conversations when they showed the influence of new French ideas. In his memoirs Goldoni describes how the day he became a lawyer he happened to be waiting for a gondola in his wig and toga when a well-dressed but clearly plebeian woman approached him and struck up a conversation; though he had never seen her before she knew his name, his place of study, his relatives. She began to offer him rather shady jobs which would bring quick money and professional fame, but he turned them down and told her that he was a man of honour. To this she made a strange reply, shaking him by the hand, 'You do well to be honourable, and I hope you will always remember our conversation and keep to what you have said.' Some time later he found out that she was a spy. But who had planted her and with what objective he never came to know. Those who planted her probably did not know either.

The capital sentences ceased to be about affairs of state. Nearly all those recorded for the previous centuries had been cases of treason, real or invented, but in the eighteenth century there are robberies and private murders involving teachers and manufacturers and officers and café proprietors; the cause is resentment, jealousy, petty vendetta. In fact, throughout the century not one treason of state is recorded. There were six capital sentences in the fourteenth century, nineteen in the fifteenth, twenty-four in the sixteenth, fifteen in the seventeenth and twenty-one in the eighteenth. This rise was due partly to the greater public order towards the end of the Republic, partly to the fact that in earlier epochs murder would have been avenged privately. The last case, in 1791, was that of Pietro Lucchese, a count from the Friuli, who hated the *podestà* of Caneva (where he lived) and with the help of an accomplice murdered him. The motive was no deeper than personal dislike.

But at the same time as there was more civic sense, there was less vigilance in law and order. The prisons were no longer efficient: criminals and madmen and children were mixed in the same cells, and lived in their excrement. Certain people could buy immunity from law: Count Alemanno Gambara, a *signorotto*, spent most of his life killing and threatening innocent people on his estate near Brescia. The Inquisitors punished him at worst with a mild and brief period of exile, and always with instructions that he should be treated well. Too weak to administer their own order, they may have felt grateful for his effective personal dictatorship in one of their own provinces, even when he beat up or murdered their *sbirri*, and intercepted their taxes on the way from Brescia (leaving a polite note of thanks for a year's revenue).

Survival had become more important to the aristocracy than an impeccably ordered state. The police were now bribable. The healthiest cells were sold to criminals with most money. A tavern was set up in

....

the prison, and murder and robbery went on all the time. The kind of police order that Napoleon brought was urgently required. And the state, that is the aristocracy, fell over itself to give way to him for this reason above any other. After his entry men like Manin, the rich but not blue-blooded class, could sleep soundly in their beds, without fear of a popular rising.

The quality of the doges went down. Good men no longer relished the job, always an empty one, and in any case the electors usually opposed good men. Money had always, since at least the fourteenth century, changed hands in a ducal election. But now money was the only influence. Venice was being sucked dry to keep its aristocracy at the gambling tables. Expenses for the nineteen-day election went up from about seventy thousand lire at the beginning of the century to at least four hundred thousand at the end, with the steepest rises in the second half of the century. Paolo Renier, elected in 1779, is said to have been corrupt as a matter of nature, and to have bribed more extravagantly than any previous doge: he sweetened not only the Barnabotti but the common people outside (their favourite for the dogeship was a Venier). He sold state offices and even licences to beg at the doors of the Basilica. Yet he was a brilliant orator, a brilliant man altogether. He saw Venice's collapse coming. He also kept a lover from Constantinople in luxury, and may have been privately married to her: Margherita had once been a rope dancer, and both inside and outside the ducal palace she was known as the 'dogaressa', though that position was officially taken by the doge's niece Giustina Michiel Renier. Goethe was present at Margherita's trial over a deed of trust, and described it as a comedy even better than the one he had seen the previous evening at the S. Moisè theatre. It went off like a stage production, naturally and unfussed, for the good reason that everything had been decided beforehand and both sides knew what to expect. Margherita he described as 'enveloped in her *cendà*', handsome, in fact noble, her expression serious if not sad. The Venetians, he said, were particularly proud that such a highly placed woman (whom he took to be the actual dogaressa) should be on trial in her own palace. It was all theatre, really – Goethe was quite right: the

I

trial, the pride in annoying the doge were only echoes from an austere past, amusing, done for effect now.

Doge Renier's death was kept secret for some days because of the carnival: no one wanted to stop the enjoyment for such an un-lamented end. He died slowly ; people said that his soul refused to leave without being paid first. That was the atmosphere of the city in 1789. He was buried without fuss in S. Niccolò dei Tolentini.

The Republic had been thought impregnable and inexhaustibly wealthy for so long that even her leading subjects milked her when-ever they could. At the end of the eighteenth century she was therefore many times weaker than she need have been; a state declines because its people gives up, not because of circumstances, which have an astonishing flexibility under a strong will. Throughout the cen-tury there was an atmosphere of drift. The army cost as much as it had always done but its numbers had dwindled, so that what on paper was a regiment might mean a platoon on the ground. Corfu was de-fended on paper by one company of Venetians and two of Albanians, but the whole force consisted of a couple of Venetian officers (who drew pay for the whole lot). Names on pay-rolls remained perpetual, irrespective of death and lapsed contract. A live soldier who actually got his pay would often take service with another state and never be found out. A fortune went down the drain this way.

The Arsenal was a thorough mess, though it continued to have the full complement of men, and cost if anything more to run than in the previous century. Its guild-laws were disregarded. Most of the work-men only turned up for pay-day, and there was no check on the number of their attendances. Some of them took other jobs, while getting full pay. They used the wood meant for ship-building to warm their homes : a government inspector of 1784 said that for some years about seventy thousand faggots had disappeared annually in this way. The apprentices (sons of the workmen, by guild law) paid for their certificates of entry instead of studying for them : that is, they paid for their right to get a life-long salary for doing nothing. When Napoleon cleared out the Arsenal he found most of the ships badly fitted, and some not even sea-worthy.

The hired troops used to maintain order in the mainland provinces were useless. The band of Croatians in charge of Padua was too inefficient to defend itself against an attack by students. As for the colonial outposts their defences were all but decayed: draw-bridges rusted over, battlements were overgrown with bushes and trees; those guns which had not rusted up were without carriages.

The ordinary Venetian almost certainly never realised the real state of affairs, in his prolonged daydream. Things had been managed so well and for so long above his head that he could not realise he was no longer provided for. 'They' would see to it all. A few men at the top – on whom it all depended – did try to take things in hand but their complaints drifted away down the canals with the tide. Angelo Emo, who had seen the English and Dutch fleets and had travelled widely, argued for urgent reform, but no one listened. Only his unfashionable firmness kept the war against the Bey of Tunis going in 1784: he won, and thereby curbed piracy in colonial waters. But France was the gainer here, as Louis XVI tactitly acknowledged when he wrote a letter of thanks to the doge Manin. Some say that Emo was poisoned by his second-in-command, who succeeded him.

Chapter 10

The City of Music

If there was one thing that soothed the titillated nerves and made up – for a moment – for the collapse of seriousness it was music. Venice was mad for it. If the soul was locked away, music opened it. The creature paused. It was true of all classes. Whether it was a concert, a Mass or a gondolier exchanging stanzas of Tasso across the lagoon at night –

> *Fummo un tempo felici*
> *Io amante ed amato,*
> *Voi amata ed amante in dolce stato –*

it was always a reminder of something like religion. Music made the Venetian faint with pleasure. It embodied all that religion had once given him; it captured the old peace, the firmness, the sense that all things were composed into their proper shape for a moment.

There was a concert every evening. The best music came from the four charitable institutions, the Mendicanti, the Pietà, the Incurabili and the Ospedaletto, where orphan-girls (meaning illegitimate children) had their principal education at the state's expense. They played all instruments, are said to have sung like angels. A girl called Zabetta (of the Incurabili) had a frenzied following among ordinary people; so did Margarita of the Mendicanti. The best symphonies came from the Pietà, where Chiaretta the violinist played; she and a girl called Anna Maria were said to be two of the finest soloists in the peninsula. Some foreigners found the sight of a female orchestra amusing. Beckford did: 'The sight of the orchestra still makes me smile. You know, I suppose, it is entirely of the feminine gender, and that nothing is more common than to see a delicate white hand journeying across an enormous double bass, or a pair of roseate cheeks puffing, with all their efforts, at a French horn. Some that are grown old and Amazonian, who have abandoned their fiddle and their lovers, take vigorously to the kettle-drum ; and one poor limping lady, who had been crossed in love, now makes an admirable figure on the bassoon.' And Mrs Thrale found the idea of girls 'handling the double bass and blowing into the bassoon' unpleasing, and the choice of a mezzo-soprano to sing Saul 'an odd, unnatural thing enough'. But she loved the girls, their 'seducing manners and soft address', in the parlour afterwards.

No Venetians found it funny or odd, as of course it was not. While the theatre was a place for fun and intrigue, the concert hall meant a grave refinement. This did not mean an absence of scandal: after the music the girls mingled with the audience for chocolate, flirting and assignations. But for the music there was awed attention, which Beckford mentions in another paragraph: 'Every tribune was thronged with people, whose profound silence showed them worthy auditors of this master's music. Here were no cackling old women, or groaning Methodists, such as infest our English tabernacles, and scare one's ears with hoarse coughs, accompanied by the *naso obligato*. All were still and attentive.' Some of the concerts, like this one, were given in church. Mass sometimes lasted five hours, and was rehearsed exhaustively. Six orchestras were once used for High Mass at St Mark's, under Galuppi's direction. Rousseau said he knew nothing in the world to touch the music of the orphans ; Goethe had never heard such voices as those of the Mendicanti girls, nor anything so voluptuous and moving as the music they sang.

On holidays the Venetians usually went to the Incurabili for their Vespers : at the beginning of the century two of the novices there, Greghetta and Anzoletta, were said not to 'chant' the vespers so much as to 'enchant'. Again and again these girls carried their audiences to the edge of an unbearable exhilaration. People would cry, shake their heads, lose themselves in ecstasy. The girls at the Pietà, according to Dr Burney, who travelled the whole of Italy for his general history of music, 'played a thousand tricks in singing, particularly in the duets, where there was a trial of skill and of natural powers, as who could go highest, lowest, swell a note the longest, or run divisions with the greatest rapidity.'

Music was a natural power in Venice, inherited by people of every class. The first music Burney heard there was in the street, immediately on his arrival, 'performed by an itinerant band of two fiddlers, a violincello, and a voice, who, though as unnoticed here as small-coalmen or oyster-women in England, performed so well, that in any other country of Europe they would not only have excited attention, but have acquired applause, which they justly merited.' Once Beckford and a friend took 'provisions and music' to the low desert isles beyond Mazerbo, and played 'several delightful airs, that called forth the inhabitants of every island, and held them in silence, as if spell-bound, on the edge of their quays and terraces, till we were out of hearing.' When they played at one of the island convents the nuns stared from their cells, weeping, and the old abbess told them afterwards that the music had seemed to come 'from the gates of paradise ajar'.

Venice sent teachers all over Europe, teachers of singing, the violin, harmony. Domenico Scarlatti, Porpora, Hasse, Jomelli, Sacchini taught at the four *conservatoires*. But the Venetians were not only served by skilful musicianship. There was a distinctive Venetian music, poured forth year after year by many composers – light, spontaneous, clear as water, delighting in itself as much as the painters delighted in their medium.

To us it must look as if, with such ready and superbly appreciative audiences, the composers only had to write the music down. That was not the case. Cimarosa was carried through the streets in triumph one night: the composer of a successful opera was the greatest man in the city – but only for a day or two. Concentration was the least of Venice's powers. A known pleasure was a dead one. Otherwise it would have been impossible for Vivaldi, a born Venetian, a much greater composer than the craze for him a few years ago gave him credit for, could not have died in poverty, more or less forgotten. Perhaps only J. A. Hasse, the Saxon whose work is rarely performed today, was more than Venice's rage of the hour. But that may have been because

....

he married the singer Faustina Bordoni, whom Rosalba painted and whose name was enough to bring a hush on any conversation.

Music had always been strangely congenial to Venice, the city of water. For one thing it had been a necessary accompaniment, and sometimes the climax, of so many state and church occasions; and church occasions had always been lavish state affairs too – that was the Venetian policy of outdoing papal Rome in pomp, so as to seem its equal, in control of the spiritual side. Motets, cantatas, passions, oratorios had always gone with the vivid robes and banners, the jewelled *zentildonne*, the glittering ambassadorial gondolas and silk-draped boats, the processions that wound round St Mark's Square, almost as if music was a comment from the water itself, a floating element, heard as the water was seen, at every corner yet insubstantial. That was why Venice had perhaps the finest musical tradition in Europe.

The first important polyphonic school started there at the beginning of the sixteenth century as a child of the earlier Flemish school, under Willaert, who became chapel master at St Mark's in 1527, after studying with Josquin des Prés in Paris. It was he who founded its singing school. That, together with what was happening under Palestrina and Victoria in Rome, was what we call the Renaissance in music. Andrea Gabrielli took over Willaert's post, and in 1585 his nephew, Giovanni, followed him, after serving at the Duke of Bavaria's court for a time.

Just as Venice stimulated her painters to a wonderful self-assurance, a repose that went right through their technique, so in music she achieved an unmistakeable quality of her own; repose and balance and clarity are what we notice most. We hear it in Giovanni Gabrielli's motet *O Jesu me dolcissime*, with its elaborate simplicity, its unhurried, tender, solemn flow, the outcome of recognised craftsmanship supported by the vast power of state. That motet is also a chromatic madrigal, namely a musical setting of a poem, contrapuntal in style: we are hearing something which is no longer simply and narrowly (it was now felt to be narrow) sacred music, but an outburst of feeling not so different from what you would expect in a pastoral or love song. The word 'Renaissance' here means precisely the same as in painting – the secularisation of sacred subjects and forms: not their rejection but their explanation, so to speak, in terms of daily life. In painting the actual movements of people are studied, their clothes and their buildings; Christ and the Virgin become real; their suffering is real. The stylised elements of the earlier art disappear: the artists, depicting individuals for the first time, become individuals themselves. The same happens in music: and it is Monteverdi who achieves a clear secular message for the first time, in his *Vespers* on the one hand and his operas on the other; religious struggle moves into daily life, and daily life moves into the Church, through the vehicle of art. At one time all musical drama was sacred: but the Renaissance divided it into what we now call the oratorio (where the musical drama is no longer acted) and the new secular drama, with its arias and duets, which came to be known as opera.

Really Monteverdi's *Vespers*, written after he had become chapel master at St Mark's in 1613, was the climax of the work done by the Gabrielli; they almost break into the later oratorio form, into Passion music and the 'concert mass' of the eighteenth century. After Monteverdi, the devotional side of church music gradually became the 'absolute music' of the concert as we know it, while the dramatic elements (the story of Christ or the saints) became opera. The eighteenth century was the epoch in which the secularisation of music was realised to a point where people listened to it with *devotional* attention, of the kind they would once have given only to a church piece.

Music came to be associated with the senses in precisely the same way as painting did, during this baroque period. And the word baroque is used about seventeenth- and eighteenth-century music in the same way. But whereas in painting it comes to mean some insincerity under cover of craftsmanship – the *tour de force* taken to a fanatical extreme of posturing and emptiness – in music it can mean no such thing. Far from being a collapse from earlier musical values, eighteenth-century music was a climax of them, in a way that baroque painting was certainly not a climax of the early Sienese or Florentine work. Far from being a period of decline, a fall from Monteverdi, a pause before the great Viennese masters, it was the first triumphant exercise of music for pleasure. That idea itself – art for pleasure – was certainly a decline of values, but the music went a long way beyond sensual appeasement. Vivaldi and Albinoni and Marcello turned the pleasure to something new, even mystical, and this was later developed to fullness in Mozart. None of what we call classical music would have been possible without those composers of eighteenth-century Venice. Far from being a period of decadence it was one of fervid preparation.

But it remains that the drawbacks of the Italian style were over-decoration and the worship of the *tour de force*; if baroque means simply the tyranny of the virtuoso, then it certainly does apply to Venetian work in the eighteenth century. The composers north of the Alps (beginning with Schütz, who studied under Giovanni Gabrielli) were fired by Italian styles but recoiled from their extravagances: that was how 'classical' music came into being.

The concert as we know it developed at this time, a type of music which was not a song and told no story, yet was also not an oratorio, a motet or a setting of a psalm. It was a comment on life in music, an evocation; and a group of people actively listened to it as if it told a story. It was a musical exposition of life, even an adoration; yet not tied to the liturgy. Music became a free, pure medium ('absolute' music for the first time); in Venice it was a blissful evocation of the order that still lay just under the surface of Venetian life.

The actual word *concerto* (or consort, 'playing-together') was first used at the end of the sixteenth century to describe sacred music involving two choirs, a 'church cantata'. Then it was used by Ludovico Viadana in 1622 for a number of motets for organ and voice (*concerti ecclesiastici*). Sixty years later it took on an orchestral form in a piece for two violins and figured bass by Giuseppe Torelli, really a *sonata da camera*. But it was Arcangelo Corelli who first created a real orchestral concerto, towards the end of the seventeenth century. He had already made himself known as a violin virtuoso at the age of nineteen, in 1672. His Opus 6, with its series of *concerti* for two violins, 'cello and accompaniment (*concertino obligato*) was the model for the later *concerto grosso*, or 'big consort'. In his hands it became a form where a small group of solo instruments (*concertino*) was joined to the rest of the orchestra in an equivalent of *chiaroscuro* in painting, a contrast of light and shade. And in the era of the virtuoso, a century later, the *concerto* became, very often, what we mean by it today, a solo instrument against an orchestral background; it settled into three movements, *adagio-presto-adagio*. Corelli's *concerti* had a great influence, chiefly on Vivaldi, who in more than four hundred *concerti* undertook what was more or less a purification of musical form, after the polyphony of the previous epoch. And he in turn was perhaps the deepest influence on Bach.

Handel too heard Corelli's music in Italy, and published a set of twelve *concerti grossi*. The modern word 'concert', to describe a programme of music distinct from a 'recital' of solo instruments, came into use for the simple reason that the *concerto* was the basis of the new classical music, brought to perfection by Haydn and Mozart. It meant too the triumph of the violin, as a basis of almost all composition. The sonata and chamber music generally were aspects of the same transition, and they too were developed by Corelli.

In Tomaso Albinoni, too, the *concerto*, with or without soloist, came to an exquisite fulfilment. The Venetians could never have been bored in their concert halls, they were given such variety – not only in the daily change of bill but the musical piece itself. Each movement of his *Concerto a Cinque in C Major* is clearly marked from the other, without a phrase wasted or irrelevant; the two Allegro movements are quite distinct expressions, the first of order, the second of a pleasant gay abandon, while the Adagio in between stirs a particularly Venetian kind of sadness – gracious, fine, reflective, but with a firmness that prevents any suggestion of over-refinement. The other *Concerto a Cinque in C Major* (Opus 5, number 12) has the same accepted three-movement form: it begins with an ordered presentation, thrilling because of the subtle way it seems to defy its own strict form. (Here in fact is half the excitement of the best, as also of the worst, music of that time – the rapturous liberties it took with its own powerful structures.) This is followed by the reflective pause, never self-indulgent, of the Adagio, which enters straight into a complicated

Presto of a decorative kind. And the last movement is one of release, brisk in pace, triumphantly lacking in hesitation.

The courage of Venetian music at that time lay in its insistence on order and grace at all times, its refusal of suffering as anything but a medium to rapture. When you hear Cimarosa's little *Concerto in C Major* for oboe, with its ease and subtle assurance, its superb dancing rhythm, the sense it gives of unswerving authority, and the tenderness that is allowed, so to speak, to seep through the authority, you no longer wonder at Venetians fainting when they heard him. Though not born in Venice, he was in many ways a climax of its baroque powers.

A comparison of Venetian music at this time with, say, Handel's would show up the latter's spirituality ; he has a softer, more solemn, more lingering touch. The Venetians are brilliant, endlessly effective, carelessly expert, rapturous, original, striking, turning the *tour de force*, so demanded by the fashions of the time, to serious use.

Above all in Antonio Vivaldi, whose dates are about the same as Albinoni's, covering almost the first half of the eighteenth century, you have an ecstatic, daring exploration which seems to be about to bring the whole form crashing down but only confirms it the better for the risk. He produced two sets of *concerti grossi*, the first (Opus 3) called *L'Estro Armonico* ('Harmonic Inspiration') with twelve pieces, and the second set, Opus 8, called *Il Cimento dell'Armonia e dell' Invenzione* or 'The Proof of Harmony and Invention' (a typical Venetian ideal), which includes a quartet of *concerti* called *The Four Seasons*, the earliest example of what we now call programme music.

In his *Concerto in D minor* for viola d'amore and lute he mutes the violins, making a strange, lively, thoroughly fresh combination. The plucking of the lute is a perfect, intimate support for the singing tone of the viola d'amore. And in another way his *Concerto in G major* for two mandolins, strings and continuo is intriguing, bubbling with invention. But in all human production there is nothing more unbearably lovely than the *Adagio* movement of his *Concerto in D major* for piccolo, where all the serenity of his city is caught, glittering like the water, still like the lagoon, as if music had passed beyond itself to nature, beyond nature to an independent being: there is such peace in it that it hardly seems possible for the medium to be music or anything concrete at all. Its most daring little runs in no way disturb the form, or the sense that music has in the strangest way been surpassed.

In his *Four Seasons* there is the same pervasion of light, a happiness that is not just joy but a celebration of clarity and health, the wonder that so much splendour can exist between the earth and sky. Each of the seasons is a study in itself, a whole *concerto* in the accepted three-movement form, and personifies the baroque description of life: there is no longer dance or song, the listeners are no longer participants; they simply witness an evocation in sound. The audience in the modern sense has come into being. Every movement of the *Seasons* is a riot of colour and light: there are birds, rushing and serene winds, barking dogs, a pleasant country dance, the tired grumbling of peasants, the pleasurable oppression of summer heat; there are wasps and flies, thunder and lightning; we feel the winter air that cuts and stimulates. The singing and dancing contained here are no longer an end in themselves: they are depicted; music is now the art of evocation, has even moved close to literature.

Vivaldi's whole composition is pervaded by a rushing fluency: his *La Stravaganza* of 1712, probably part of a work composed ten years before when he was in his early twenties, shows the ease that is going to be deployed later in every direction. As a priest he was obliged to give up celebrating Mass because of chronic asthma. Yet there is never a breath of self-indulgence in his work, never a suggestion that art is a private activity. Until his thirties he wrote mostly instrumental music, as teacher and violinist at the Pietà. Then between 1718 and 1722 he began to travel and write operas. He returned to the Pietà but, famous now, worked more on his own compositions than before. And in 1740 he left Venice for Vienna, where he died. He was disappointed perhaps at the response of the Venetian public. They did not always faint at the loveliest music. They applauded like mad, but taste was mostly a matter of current convention, that is fashion, which makes the worst climate for an artist to work in.

Venice gave endless opportunities for musical performances, but finally the masquerade prevailed, which is why she went maddest over the *opera buffa*.

Vivaldi had a vast output: four hundred *concerti* for various solo instruments, fifty-three sonatas and nearly the same number of church-pieces, with about forty operas. His first piece was dedicated to Corelli, the great name in music at the end of the seventeenth century. Corelli was closer to Monteverdi than to any of the eighteenth-century composers: his work is measured, delicate, with the variety of form that became a necessary characteristic of the later music, but without any suggestion of the *tour de force*. The unhinged, wildly happy tone of the later music is missing; there is none of the fervid sense of release. In its place is absolute seriousness; the music is not being sacrificed to *virtuoso* considerations. In the later music there is an excitement that seems to be leading towards destruction, to the collapse of the nervous system: Vivaldi's period was a last fling of serenity and sound enjoyment.

The idea of the *concerto* began in church: the congregation became the concert-audience, only they went to a hall or a private house for it. Tartini, for instance, who really introduced the violin to Venice as the basis of most composition, used to play excerpts from his *concerti* during Mass at S. Antonio in Padua, where he was master of music. The act of adoration therefore left the church: and the lay-concert became as far from anything liturgical as the opera. And in this new delightful freedom there was the menace of formlessness: the element of destruction lay there, a first shadow of northern romantic music. Once the liturgy was left behind, and the philosophy of religion abandoned as a basis of life, only the lonely and distraught figure of the artist himself remained. And that was another beginning. Sometimes in baroque music it seems that we have already reached that point, long before we are in fact there. It is found in the hushed and ominous entrance of Vivaldi's *Second Concerto in G minor*, which is so near Beethoven; it is hinted at again in the Largo movement, to be swept away in a smacking Allegro as a finale; balance and clarity have won, if only by a neck. It is there too in his solo *Domine Deus, Agnus Dei* with the choral interpolation of *Qui tollis peccata mundi* (from the

Gloria): we are passing beyond the form to a disaster (the music makes a sudden reflective pause in the hurried act of writing).

The baroque period presented a wonderful fruit, fully ripe, but in a moment it was rotten.

Baldassare Galuppi once said to Dr Burney that music had to have *vaghezza, chiarezza e buona modulazione* – 'grace, clarity and good modulation'. While music stayed at this safe anchorage no collapse was possible. But gradually the nervous system ceased to be capable of it: the old harmony of nerves was breaking down, and with it musical harmony naturally broke down too. The nineteenth century was a successive destruction of those principles of Galuppi's. And how far the collapse had taken place towards the end of the Republic can be seen from the fact that Vivaldi was unknown at his death. His church pieces, like his operas, remained unplayed. It was Bach who rescued his work for us. His *Gloria* was only found in the '30s of this century.

Monteverdi had produced his *Orpheus* in 1607. This not only brought opera into being, that is, the unfolding of a story in terms of music; it began the possibility of serious lay-music, as opposed simply to songs and dances, for the first time. His Prologue began:

> *Io la Musica son, ch'ai dolci accenti,*
> *So far tranquillo ogni turbato core,*
> *Ed or di nobil ira ed or d'amore*
> *Poss' infiammar le più gelate menti.*

'I am Music; with sweet accents I know how to make every disturbed heart quiet, and I can inflame the coldest minds with noble anger or with love.' Here the neo-classical Tragedy comes into music for the first time. If music as serious dramatic description could be said to have had a beginning, it would be in the terrible news of Eurydice's death, brought to the happy Orpheus by a messenger: the hushed *'La tua diletta sposa è morta'* ('your lovely wife is dead') brings his delight to a sudden end; until this point his joy has been pagan, celebrated with pastoral dances and songs, supported by the implicit belief that the flesh is everything, that triumph endures. He lets out a brief, broken *'Ohimé!'*, and her replying aria *'In un fiorito prato'*, describing how his bride was bitten by a snake when picking flowers, is sung in a great hush, usually with the simple accompaniment of a lute. From that point in the opera the musical form is bent to the needs of the drama ; and the drama is not simply an empty exercise in tension ; it is the exposure of Orpheus' delight as pagan, that is, as of small mystical insight. And the story of this opera, the point of the drama, is Orpheus' gradual winning of mystical insight, until he recognises that there is a certain godly delight which cannot be celebrated, and is beyond the reach of sadness. The woodwind now displaces the strings as the main vehicle of exposition. The truth has broken through the veil of classical day-dreaming ; religion has overtaken the pagan enslavement to the here-and-now. The 'melodrama' with its tiresome neo-classical subjects and lavish spectacle has become a real experience.

When Monteverdi settled in Venice in 1613 he brought opera with him, and twenty-four years later the first public opera house known was opened at the S. Cassiano theatre. In the next decade or so thirty different operas were produced, mostly by Monteverdi and his followers, the chief of whom was Francesco Cavalli. In Cavalli's work the aria became more expansive and expressive, a hint of what it would be in the eighteenth century – a vehicle for the virtuoso. He was the first to use the word 'opera' as a description of this new, rather hotch-potch form of theatre. *Opera scenica* simply meant a group of scenic works strung together, and it was a useful way of denoting the variety of the new form, especially as it developed later – a mixture of duet, aria, quartet, chorus, with the orchestra providing an overture in the three-movement form of the *concerto*, and *intermezzi* or stop-gap comic pieces (usually a two-act *opera buffa*), filling the intervals while the scenes were changing.

It was with Alessandro Scarlatti in Naples that the new form came into its full modern flush, which in turn had repercussions on Venetian opera : the *aria da capo* (an aria in three parts where the last part went 'from the beginning' again), ensemble singing, the overture, the three-act convention, the emphasis on the singer and his song rather than on the meaning of the drama were all developed in his work. He, more than the earlier Venetian school, was the main influence on the eighteenth-century Venetians – Jomelli, Porpora, Galuppi. By their time opera had become a glorious game, with the most elaborate scenic techniques which would astonish a modern producer with his revolving stages and light-dipping apparatus. The aria became a sort of sports-event for the Italian audience, until by the nineteenth century it was a nuisance: Verdi dispensed with it in his *Othello*, thereby declaring himself master of the opera and not vice versa. In eighteenth-century Venice there was no question who was master: it was certainly not the composer.

Clearly Monteverdi's *Orpheus* was the kind of thing that could never have flourished in the Venice of that time. Though it was performed and though it delighted, being a natural part of any theatre's repertoire, it remained apart. The classical mania went on, in music, rather as if nothing had happened, or rather as if Monteverdi had only produced a new bag of tricks: Metastasio the librettist was, so to speak, the acknowledged lion of the mania, even as far as Vienna. One classical theme after another was exploited in grandiose and spectacular affairs which had to surprise the audience as well as satisfy the hard demands of the virtuosi. It is very doubtful if eighteenth-century Venice would even have liked Monteverdi's opera had it been produced for the first time a century later than it was. Venice's taste was for music that skated inconsequentially along, where the virtuosi could show themselves off without disturbing the casual plot. The seed lay in Pergolesi's *La Serva Padrona*, which he produced in Naples in 1733 as an intermezzo for a serious opera of his, *Il Prigioniero Superbo*, which was as much of a flop as his comic intermezzo was a triumph. It was the basis of most of the work of Galuppi, Cimarosa, Paisiello. Its speed and perfectly aimed shafts of humour were exactly in the tone of modern Venice.

Pergolesi's musicalisation of Goldoni's little piece achieved in the comic exactly what Monteverdi had done in the tragic: the music became the very meaning of the words. The servant Serbina's replies to Uberto, saucy, provoking, subtle, fitted the humour of the time perfectly. A pleasing balanced power was what people asked for in the form, and this they certainly got from his piece. Serbina's aria '*Stizzoso mio stizzoso !*' in which she tells her master to shut up, is bright, sailing, happy. The superb Goldoni stroke of having a mute as the third character, to whom Uberto addresses his impotent indignation, makes it all a superbly rounded construction. The duet where she asks him for a 'yes, yes' to marriage between them and he insists on 'no, no' has a tenderness in the argument which goes through all the best *opera buffa* of the eighteenth century. It is one of those theatrical productions that seem to have acclaim written into them, a special *éclat* that one catches at once, sweeping everything – orchestra, singers, audience – into an unhesitating unity for as long as it lasts.

Baldassare Galuppi wrote three or four *opere buffe* a year for Venice, most of them on libretti by Goldoni ; and in all he wrote about seventy operas, as well as Masses, psalms, oratorios, motets and madrigals. Catherine of Russia once invited him to her court at a salary of four thousand rubles a year. The delight that poured from his music, the unhesitating spontaneity of one phrase galloping after another as if doubt had never existed in the world, the brilliant clarity, the lightness that seems to be a defiance – a firm unravelling of tortuous problems – made him famous everywhere. His strings-writing is clear and defining, almost like a voice. When he is gay the music plunges along as if it must upset itself, but never does. Each of the arias is a new departure, producing a fresh delight, with *pizzicato* accompaniment, or over mourning strings. Or they are quick and fascinating, gone too soon, with wonderfully modulated rhythms, as in *Il Filosofo di Campagna*. Here was a servant of Venice, if there ever was one.

He wrote without stopping for fifty years, and when Burney met him in his old age he found him still fresh and witty. Problems never seemed to exist for him, which of course means that he brought his craft to such maturity that he could be smooth and blithe all the time. That was what Venice loved ; that was why he was perhaps her most adored servant in music. He learned under Lotti, and started as a harpsichord player. Then he became choirmaster at the Basilica, and

K

afterwards director of the Incurabili. Every one of the seven theatres in the city was virtually his home by the middle of the century.

But only the satisfaction of a ready audience, and his own inclination towards their tastes, could have made it bearable. The demands of the time were very limited after all: which is why the music seems so often defiant, as if obstinately projecting its passion through the dictatorial form. Benedetto Marcello, a composer of noble birth (therefore never a professional musician) who studied under Lotti and Gasparini and translated Dryden's *Timotheus* for one of his own solo cantatas, parodied it all in his little book *Teatro alla Moda*. It gives bogus advice to musicians, virtuosi, writers, as to how to put over a successful work. A magnificent scene, he says, must be stuck in at the end of the opera to make everyone gasp (and to stop them leaving in the middle). A writer must never imitate the 'obscure, tedious and bitter' poets like Dante, Petrarch, Ariosto. The plot must never be clear and understandable, otherwise it will be thought trite, and it should be dedicated to some great personage who also happens to be rich. For this dedication an intermediary should be used, if only the other man's cook. In the dedication the patron's family should be exalted together with his ancestors, using the words 'liberality' and 'generous spirit' as often as possible. If you could think of nothing to praise in him you should say you did not wish to offend his modesty by reciting his virtues.

To the musicians Marcello's advice was, 'Know the rules'. The arias should be one gay and one pathetic, without regard to words, meaning or convenience of the scene. When there was a cadenza the orchestra leader should stop all the instruments and let the virtuoso go on as long as he liked. Musicians should compose scores with many errors in them, and as carelessly as possible, so as to satisfy the audience. They should slow the tempo for virtuosi, hiding their indiscretions, because their own reputations depended on the virtuosi alone. Musicians should never compose arias with *basso solo obligato*, since in the same amount of time they could compose a dozen instrumental pieces. If the virtuosi or their 'protectors' (all the singers had their noblemen in train who elected themselves protectors) did not like an aria a musician should tell them that the thing had to be sung on the actual night, under the lights, before a live audience, to be really effective. And to the players and singers Marcello advised, 'If you do an aria badly or don't get applause, blame it on the aria and say it wasn't "theatrical".' Just as a libretto had to provide five arias – two in the first act, two in the second and one in the third – so a symphony could only be composed under the strictest rules ; it had to have so-called French time. or a *prestissimo* of semiquavers in major, succeeded by a *piano* of the same key in minor, and ending in a minuet, gavotte or jig in the major ; fugues, *legature*, themes, were regarded as quite out.

So what we have left of Venice's music – unswervingly graceful, clear, well-modulated, as Galuppi wanted it – is what survived the ruins, what managed by sheer brilliance to get through bad theatre. The audience was so undiscriminating – while being perhaps the most dis-criminating audience in the world on technical matters – that the good was swept into the theatres and concert halls with the bad. As long as it was music, it had a good chance, so hungry was the city's daily need, with seven theatres opening every evening of the week, and con-certs in private houses, in churches and halls, and music needed for processions, state banquets, coronations.

Marcello, who lived at the beginning of the century (he died in Brescia in 1739), liked to define himself as a musical dilettante ; the word was not pejorative at the time ; he simply meant what Dostoevsky meant when he said he was not a professional writer. Marcello was well-read ; an intelligent humanism shines through his music, with its compassionate, unhindered, sincere flow. It is in fact rare music for eighteenth-century Venice. Perhaps of all the composers of that time he escaped the close demands made on the composers by the audiences. It is even difficult to call his music baroque. His form has an inevitability, an harmonious self-assurance as if he needed to draw nothing from his audience. Without his little book we would hardly know what a triumph all the best Venetian music was over its audiences.

....

Chapter 11

Literary Lions
and 'Il Gran Goldoni'

Opera was really a matter of music coming to the rescue of literature. The literary people failed to produce tragedy. The pieces they did produce failed to stand on their own feet as theatrical presentations.

You could say that the neo-classical mania in Italy destroyed the possibility of a literature, were it not for the fact that the same mania in other countries caused and nourished it. But then Italy never had a literature. She had poets, who came and went. Her poetry was stirred into being by St Francis, as his was in turn by the French *chansons* ; and the same root of chivalry brought Italy's first love poets to the court of the Hohenstaufen, Frederick II, in Sicily. Unlike France (and her political offspring, England) Italy had no monarch in whom all power and loyalty were centralised : she lacked the sources of a literature, which by definition is more than provincial. Petrarch showed that he was quite aware of this when he tried, again and again, and always unsuccessfully, to teach the Venetians, the Genoese, the Milanese that they were the same sort of people not only as each other (a horrible enough thought for any of them) but as Romans and Neapolitans, because they spoke the same language. This made no impression on the courts. They listened to him and, like his friend the doge Dandolo, simply praised his prose style. The result was that the poetry and plays became more and more just that – style. The serious use of classical models in Petrarch's time, the careful editing of classical texts at the Aldine press (the italic script it invented is said to have been a copy of Petrarch's handwriting) dwindled into manner and artificiality. You have a hint of it, a certain rhetorical evasion of the truth, even in Petrarch.

Perhaps a literature, that is an inherited language, changed by every writer while remaining in the most uncanny way its unmistakable self, needs a real society to bring it into being. Its language has to be the language of daily life. And in Italy, as in Germany – another country divided into self-governing duchies – the two languages, that of writing and that of daily speech, tended to become more and more disparate. That was how Tuscan became Italy's national property as a language : it was a necessity, made possible in the first place by the poets, by Dante and Petrarch and Tasso and Ariosto, who spoke it.

But Venice *was* a society, formed from ancient roots, close-knit, ideal for novels and plays, yet without either. In fact Venice seemed to suffer from the obsession with classical models more than most other places in Italy. It meant that a poetical language, namely Tuscan dialect, was stuck on top of her own language, though her own language was an ideal vehicle for a literature.

Neo-classical clubs flourished everywhere in Italy at this time, with their elegies on the death of pet poodles, their impromptu odes on bottles of maraschino (Innocenzo Frugoni, the lyrical poet of the court of Parma, was guilty of that), their queer Arcadian 'nature' which had no dirt or toil in it, their 'poetical' pseudonyms. Pietro Trapassi, who wrote many if not most of the operas seen in Venice during the eighteenth century, was given the Greek rendering of his name (meaning 'step forwards' or 'transition') by his teacher Gravina : and he never called himself anything but Metastasio.

Surprisingly, the Arcadian clubs were a reaction against the excessive artificial classicism of the previous century ; the first club had come into being in Rome in 1690, at the little court of Queen Christina of Sweden, and its affiliated clubs spread everywhere in the peninsula, and stayed the whole of the eighteenth century. In the south the clubs were melancholy ; in Tuscany their taste went towards the burlesque ; in Lombardy they had a certain nordic seriousness. People now believed that you simply could not make poetry out of Christian and religious themes. Not even the minor, occasional verse of the period was worth preserving. In missing the religious experience, it missed the possibility of art, and any chance of being understood in later epochs. The reason why we still listen to Monteverdi's *Orpheus* as it was listened to on its first night is that he did not evade the religious experience.

The protestant countries, where people had tried to re-define religious experience, came off better: in Germany and England classicism had more of a benign influence; Shakespeare had needed little Latin and less Greek; and even Dr Johnson liked novels.

Yet Metastasio too was in reaction against the artificial kind of classicism. The whole idea of his theatre was to get something of the real tone of the Greek drama, not the literary version; his patron, Vincenzo Gravina, really started the eighteenth-century movement to bring in a genuine classicism, and one of his achievements was the revival of Dante, whose Italian had been swallowed up in avalanches of Latin. Metastasio's plays are neither mannered nor artificial. Their language is direct, simple, elegant in the best sense, Tuscan. His speeches have a note of earnest sincerity, the opposite of contrived. His plays are immobile, but he meant them to be, in the best Greek, or supposedly Greek, tradition. But there was no chance of treating a real problem in this way. The drama was taken away from the beginning. What makes Monteverdi's *Orpheus* dramatic is the fact that the story is made the vehicle of a modern problem.

And music made use of the crippling theatrical disadvantages of a classical drama that was no drama at all. Its dialogues were set to music, and 'melodrama' came into being; from being a poet Metastasio became at one stroke a librettist. The same would have happened to Goldoni had his plays not been designed for the stage, and had he not learned his tricks from the *Commedia dell'Arte*, as different from an imagined classical model as anything could be. All that the classicists knew about the ancient drama was some of the texts; they had no idea how they were acted, much less what the music (it was clear that music had been an important part of the ancient performance) had sounded like. The fifteenth-century books by Vitruvius which were greatly in vogue when the proscenium-arch type of theatre was coming into being contained mostly guesses about the classical stage, however well they defined the modern one. It was a matter of open argument. And this argument started opera.

Some people said that the ancient dialogues had been chanted against a background of music; this idea gave birth to *recitative*. Then people began to see the possibilities of a new form combining music and words even more thoroughly ; the *recitatives* would, so to speak, burst into song – the *aria* – at moments of high feeling. And Venice, above all other cities in the pensinsula, leapt at this invention as if to make up for its philistinism towards anything literary, for its having (among other things) allowed a priceless library bequeathed to it by Petrarch to literally petrify under the leads of the ducal palace. The combination of music and verse was the happiest possible one for a people who did not read much.

Whether the first opera house in the district of San Casciano had boxes is not known, but the second one in SS. Giovanni e Paolo did, as its plan (in the Sir John Soane museum in London) shows : that is to say, already at that time the opera house had become a second home for the aristocracy, a refuge from their cold and vast palazzi, where they could meet even foreigners in a casual setting. The development of opera in Venice coincided with the growing relaxation of manners.

France was a stronghold of strict classicism. There was a socially compulsive belief in the *'genres'* – a strict division of literary output into the epic, the lyric, the tragic and the comic. There was another sacred idea, that art must be didactic ; this produced some of the most painfully dull things ever printed. Plays, poems and melodramas became pre-packaged devices for passing the time of leisured people, as a background to chatter and intrigues. But gradually, even in France, the critics began to talk about imagination and feeling, in defiance of the supposedly ancient principles. In England (where Shakespeare had disregarded the principles, though it meant the neglect of his work for a couple of centuries after his death), one of the earliest plain statements of feeling or rather 'sensibility' was Richardson's *Pamela*, in 1740. At about this time Goldoni was beginning as a playwright, after a false start with two or three tragedies in the static style of Metastasio, Apostolo Zeno and Scipione Maffei. In 1750 he turned out a dramatisation of *Pamela* which was so successful with the Venetian audiences that he had to write a sequel, *Pamela Maritata* (*maritata* meaning 'married' but also, of *minestrone*, 'richly assorted').

Like England, Venice was temperamentally unsuited for the fashionable neo-classicism. They both, as maritime states, enjoyed a certain mental independence from continental Europe; their trade had brought into being downright, sensible, unclassicist middle classes with money to spend on an evening out. It was this audience Goldoni addressed; and he chose most of his characters from it. Only in him was the possibility of a real drama, a real literature, realised. Perhaps in no other part of Italy would he have had an audience; the remarkable thing is that he was not damned as vulgar. He talked the truth: not the whole truth; but this was a time when people disliked even a little bit of it. He was only allowed to give them what truth he did because he made them laugh.

The old *Commedia dell'Arte* had been a theatre of improvisation, built round definite traditional characters who followed, more or less, various expected plots. Within those limits, which had been very wide, the actors and actresses had improvised their lines. What Goldoni did was to write all the improvised lines down in the prompt book. This meant the end of improvisation, which had kept performances on a low level, with easy appeals to the easiest taste. In his 'reform', as he called his new approach to the stage, he was out to do away with the old easy, frowsty, dilapidated *actor's* theatre, where there was never a breath of outdoor life, never a problem, where every character was as predictable as the puppets in the Piazzetta. In his clear, supple lines, which cry out to be spoken, he was teaching new care to his actors. The old knockabout stuff had degraded their powers. Now they had to learn their lines. Therein lay Goldoni's appeal to the intelligent, demanding audiences that consisted of both nobles and merchants: his work needed no less subtlety and craft than the Metastasian type of theatre.

The old obscenities had to go too. After all, they had been as far removed from daily life as the grandest analogies of the neo-classical stage. His lines had to be spoken naturally: from the two opposite

....

The comedy of daily life
OPPOSITE 'Il Gran Goldoni'
OVERLEAF The barber, the tailor, the painter's workshop
and the coffee house

enemies of real theatre – knockabout improvisation on the one hand and classical declamation on the other – he rescued a lively form.

By doing this he made the Venetian audiences look at the stage with attention all the time. The story carried them along so delightfully that even their gossip seemed less important, especially as it was being done on the stage so much better than they could do it themselves.

What his plays did – and this was why he had to throw out the old improvisation – was to give a subtle and detached picture of the world round him. No lines improvised on the spot could do that. Nor were the old improvising artistes capable of saying his deft lines. His theatre was therefore a new training for the acting profession, as much as Brecht's was in Germany, Shaw's in England.

There is perhaps no figure in all Italian drama like Mirandolina in *La Locandiera*. She is quick, penetrating, sensible, scheming, beguiling, graceful, with a touch of the devil but capable of remorse and pity: a remarkable portrait, which could only have been done by a man capable of divining other people. If anything set the Venetian apart from the Italian it was this sense of the other person, a deftness in analysing their motives which made other Italians seem provincial. This is why the history of the Italian theatre really begins and ends with a Venetian, apart from the single figure of Pirandello. Having the only real society in Italy, Venice naturally had the only theatre.

Goldoni produced something like two hundred and fifty plays in forty years of work. He personified Venetian good nature. One of the truest things he ever said about himself was '*Omnia bona mea mecum porto*' – 'I carry all my luck with me.' Apart from his long period of work in the Venetian theatre he carried his luck everywhere in northern Italy, travelling as impetuously as Casanova but without ever like him calculating the main chance, only absorbing life and being tricked (especially by the women he trusted). He also said about himself that at birth he had not made a single cry, being so tranquil by nature. In his life he was a lawyer, a doctor's assistant, almost a monk and actually an ordinand; but the theatre was at the back of his mind all the time. When Cesare Darbès walked into his lawyer's office in Pisa and asked him for a comedy, he abandoned his practice

A family *in villeggiatura*

and never left the theatre again. From that time new comedies poured out, their characters chosen not from the stock creatures of the *Commedia dell'Arte* but from any disposition that happened to interest him.

Yet he sketched people ; he almost never really portrayed them. The sketches were uneven. He let out a hint and then abandoned the hint. It happened in *Todero Brontolon*, in the case of the young man Meneghetto who will marry Zanetta whatever her miserly and dictatorial grandfather, Todero, has to say about it: Meneghetto is so exact in his speech, so punctiliously elegant towards his future mother-in-law (who is on his side) that his character narrowly misses priggishness ; it makes the future mother-in-law pause for a moment to ask herself whether this young man is not dangerously like her own husband, that is, the soul of timidity. Then the hint is dropped, in the battle for Zanetta's hand – dropped in the interests of plot, movement.

Goldoni clung to facts to the point where they endangered his art : here he was quite unlike Molière, whose characters served the human drama. In a Goldoni play the likelihood of the happening is always considered, even clung to as a principle. The fact was that he wanted to give a picture of Venice, above all other dramatic considerations. Venice emerges untidy, raucous, lazily contented, with a hundred things going on at once – quarrels, assignations, legal wrangles, gossip over sewing, ardent gazing from balconies, quack medicine, lying and shouting and weeping and laughing, untamed, stinking, radiant.

In *Todero Brontolon* the old miser has a conversation with his servant Gregorio and in a few lines, his first in the play, his character is deftly established :

TODERO: Come here a minute, sir.
GREGORIO: At your service.
TODERO: You know what I've got to say to you? This: I've been in the kitchen, I've seen a damned great fire burning there, I don't get wood free, and that I won't have you going mad with it.
GREGORIO: Oh! You've been in the kitchen!

TODERO: Yessir, I have. What have you got to say?

GREGORIO: I'm not saying anything. Only that when I came in from shopping I found the fire out, the meat off the boil and I started screaming at the girl.

TODERO: Can't you boil a pot without a cartload of wood?

GREGORIO: What would you boil it with, a couple of sticks?

TODERO: Blow!

GREGORIO: I've got too much to do without standing there blowing all morning.

It is said in the crisp, cosily practical dialect. Todero's words cut, smack, undermine; like a miser, his mind always dry, he never wastes them. The climax of the little piece is 'Blow!' And this word echoes through the play. It is all his son Pellegrin is fit for, blowing. Instead of standing up for his wife against this tyrannical old skinflint, the son dashes to the kitchen – 'I'll go to the kitchen and blow!' He lives between the insults of wife and father, and is the vehicle for the transmission of insults from one to the other:

TODERO: What's happening with that idiot?

PELLEGRIN: What are you calling her an idiot for?

TODERO: Because she's an idiot: and because I'm the master of this house and say what I like: why, have you got anything to say to the contrary?

PELLEGRIN: I'm not saying anything.

Todero has his own plans for his grand-daughter: he wants her married to his steward's son, so that they can both enter his service later on. This is how he proposes it to the steward, Desiderio:

TODERO: Where's your son?

DESIDERIO: In the office, copying out a letter.

TODERO: Does the boy want to do well in life?

DESIDERIO: I think so, yes.

TODERO: And I don't think so at all.

DESIDERIO: He certainly hasn't got any vices.

TODERO: If he hasn't got them, he can always pick them up.

DESIDERIO: I don't know what to say, I don't let him get mixed up with anybody.

TODERO: How old is he?

DESIDERIO: Eighteen.

TODERO: Marry him off!

And that one word, '*maridelo*', is as forceful as 'blow', straight on the target.

Yet Goldoni never sets up opposites in his work. If a man has an exaggerated characteristic he exercises it among other people's exaggerated characteristics. No one is free of them. Nothing is simple. Todero's enemy, Marcolina, his daughter-in-law, has all our sympathy; he makes her life unbearable, as all men do who think they own the souls of those they support. But Marcolina has her characteristic as well, that of talking too much, too loudly. Goldoni watches them all, sketches them, laughs and then leaves them. A character or a situation never sweeps the picture away, in which case Venice and her people and their themes would have been lost in a moment.

We are never really swept along in a Goldoni play. We are always so much *there*, in the moment. When we finish one play we get a hunger for another, because we begin to miss his consolingly intimate scenes, as if they were now those of our own lives. Perhaps he too served Venice to the point where his art was ruined. But yet *il gran Goldoni* as the Venetians called him did not really want art. He left half the problems he stated in the air; again and again his plays read like scenarios. And this is how he conceived them. He rarely took more than eight days to write a play; when the *Comédie Italienne* in Paris gave him two months he found it difficult to spin the work out even to ten days. He was therefore much more in the *Commedia dell'Arte* tradition than at first seems likely. He found the *Commedia* theatre in total decadence: its great actors were few; the rest degraded what had once been brilliant teamwork to knockabout skit. And he revived that theatre, through himself, in a last series of brilliant sketches that happened to be written down. But Venice had a hand here simply because no other way of going to work would have been allowed him. Like the musicians he had to reckon constantly with the *virtuosi*, who wanted their funny tics and their inconvenient entrances and their *non sequitur* speeches and their pranks. Within these limits it is astonishing what he did achieve. Once when a play of his was hissed he promised the audience sixteen plays in the following year, and he gave them seventeen. He had no time to stop. A play would be thought up, written and performed all within three weeks. That was his nature too. What he did spend time on came to nothing.

At least, it came to nothing in Venice. Carlo Gozzi thought Goldoni's *Le Bourru Bienfaisant* one of his best works simply because it was clearly written with care : it did well in Paris and flopped in the Italian translation. Otherwise Gozzi thought him a poor poet, a miserable dramatist with remarkable comic gifts (especially successful in the dialect plays), strong powers of observation and abundant invention. What troubled Gozzi was the unfinished element in his work, as if a real story underneath had been left untold, and the moral issue not properly exposed. We begin with a situation, and we end with that situation resolved : the plot, the smacking pace of the dialogue, keep us too busy for thought ; we hardly notice until afterwards that the situation has not been penetrated to the real moral friction behind it. It is always a slice of life. Nor is there real drama in Goldoni. There are portraits and situations ; charity and good nature ripple through the sentences, and this is what carries us through. The inner state of his characters is left untouched. Politics, high patricians, priests and social questions are strictly outside his plays. He gives us patricians with empty pockets and broken swords because they existed and he saw them and knew them ; but beyond the sketch his interests never wandered. Carlo Gozzi, while admiring him, found the lionising of him ridiculous, because it suggested that he *did* go beyond. He rejected the inference that Goldoni was a dramatic poet, that his plays had a universal meaning subtly hidden in them. At the Arcadian club in Rome Goldoni's classical name was Polisseno Fegeio ; his first night caused the kind of excitement visiting emperors had once caused. A priest once published the news that he based his sermons on the Goldoni repertoire. Not that this meant much real respect for Goldoni. He was simply a fashion, for a fickle audience; he had to please all the time : when he failed to he was hissed.

The fact that he shared the public's attention with the *abbé* Pietro Chiari shows how much of a fashion he was. Chiari wrote long, turgid, obscure plays where the obscurity was three parts of their attraction. He looked down on Goldoni. And the city was about equally divided between them in loyalty. Carlo Gozzi attacked both. Chiari he found simply ridiculous; but even more ridiculous, he thought, was the fact that he was taken as seriously as Goldoni. He found it equally ridiculous that Goldoni should be praised for his poems, which he implied were not so much written as pissed.

This was all part of Gozzi's war to rescue language and composition from the rot that had set in all over Italy during the seventeenth century. Hack-work poured from the city's presses – bogus, forced, mannered, trying to strike the eye, relying on novelty even when the only novel thing was an unprecedented badness. It was all the product of fashion: nothing to do with real writing. It was youth showing itself off, age trying to catch the eye of youth. It was a branch of publicity. A new piece of writing had the same kind of importance as a new dress on the 'French' doll in the Merceria. It was the birth of journalism: the first gazettes and daily news-sheets belong to this period; they aired the views of one coffee house to all the other coffee houses, and made even private letters public in a matter of hours. It created an imagined world over and above the real daily one. This super-world consisted of quarrels, rumours, scandals, and included actual political news only when it could be made to look attractive, that is to say, when it had an aspect of scandal. This super-world even began to seem more real than the private one, than private thoughts. In this the eighteenth century was the crucible of the modern world; 'private' began to mean unshared by the super-world of gossip that was conjured up every day in print. And Carlo Gozzi saw what must happen as a result. It was fatal for real writing: life itself was increasingly reduced to gossip, until the demand for serious thought began to dry up.

Using a poor devil called Giuseppe Secchellari, a man eaten through with the most absurd vanity, Gozzi and a few friends started a literary club in 1740 designed to fight for purity of diction, for Dante and Petrarch and Boccaccio (whom the fashionable thought not modern enough to teach anything to the eighteenth century) and for the Tuscan language, which was also under fashionable attack. Secchellari was made its chairman and given a high throne on to which, being so short, he had to more or less jump. According to Gozzi he wrote the most appalling verse, but he was always applauded for it, and took the applause seriously (as he was meant to). In the winter he was given iced water to drink while the others had hot coffee, and in the summer boiling tea while the rest drank iced water. They put a wreath of plums round his head and called him *Arcigranellone*, meaning something like 'arch-big-ball', since the club had the burlesque title of *Accademia Granellesca* or the Testicular Academy. *Granelli*, besides meaning 'balls', also means 'fools', so that it had a double use. The club crest was an owl clutching a couple of balls in its claws. It drew as many of the fashionable youth as its enemies did. They flocked to Paolo Colombani's bookshop in the Merceria to buy the monthly *Atti Granelleschi*.

Thus the attack on Chiari and Goldoni when it came was launched from a powerful headquarters. It went on from 1757 to 1761. The impression Gozzi's memoirs give us is that Goldoni was brought down and retired to Paris hurt. The truth is that Goldoni went to Paris not only to take charge of the *Comédie Italienne* but to find a new public and perhaps new subjects. When he left, in 1761, Gozzi's plays were still new to the public.

Their literary war had all the pettiness and morose venom of literary wars in every capital of Europe at that time. Before being brought down by circumstances – by the absorption of art into the money market – writers first brought down each other. Goldoni quoted his vast following as a proof of his real value, which was a poor argument seeing that Chiari had about the same following (as well as being a poor argument anyway) ; and Gozzi pounced on this, though he used the same argument later on when *his* time came. An insipid side-effect of the war was the reconciliation between Chiari and Goldoni, who had been sworn public enemies ever since their theatrical debuts.

Had Goldoni not written something silly about Gozzi's campaign being as ineffectual as a dog barking at the moon, and had Chiari not joined him in challenging their critics to turn out a comedy which would draw as big a public as their own work, the fables of Carlo Gozzi, played for over two decades on the Venetian stages in the hands of the finest *Commedia dell'Arte* group of the time, would not have come about.

Where Goldoni's work had charmed and amused, these fairy tales beguiled and entranced and astonished ; they consisted of one exercise in the fabulous after another. There was much variety of plot and sub-plot and allegory, subtly mixed with four masques especially written in the *Commedia dell'Arte* tradition. (Goethe thought these masques the cleverest part when he saw a Gozzi fable towards the end of the century.) They drew full houses night after night and left the audiences gasping for more.

It had been one of Gozzi's main criticisms of Goldoni that he used the last decadent remains of the *Commedia dell'Arte* only to ruin it, instead of keeping it on its feet as he could and should have done. It was certainly a fact that Sacchi and his company had been obliged to leave Venice because of the Goldoni successes ; only the Lisbon earthquake had brought Sacchi back to Venice. It was this troupe that Gozzi took up and revived ; he remained loyal to them until the day years later when Sacchi left the city, no longer an actor. He gave them his scripts free. He was a patrician (his mother was a Tiepolo) and patricians at this time were deliberately amateur, deliberately useless (hence the title of his book, the 'useless memoirs'), unless they held powerful state positions. He took no money for all the hours he spent with the company, for the masses of consoling and admonitory letters he wrote to the players when they were on tour. Goldoni on the other hand exacted a high price for his comedies ; he needed the money.

Carlo Gozzi began writing for the theatre as a joke. He decided to write up an old wives' tale into a play (called *L'Amore delle Tre Melarance* or 'The Love of Three Oranges') on the grounds that the most childish nonsense, if turned out with skill, could fill a theatre. Only the fact that this deliberate joke was taken seriously made him take the theatre seriously: and then he turned out to be no more contemptuous of applause than anyone else in Venice. The vogue for his work lasted longer than that for Goldoni's (who even sent a fable-play from Paris to join in the vogue). The public was ready for a change. It gave them a new dream. Goldoni's cleverly observed scenes left contentment behind, but hardly a dream. And these child-like, quickly changing fantasies of Gozzi, drawn from every epoch, combining gods with comedy masks, shrinking the stage to the size of a table or swelling it to take in all the stars, provided everything that Goldoni had missed out. It was a last adoring look at the unsubstantial Venice that lay beneath the real one, as elusive as Venetian light.

Late in his life, in Paris, Goldoni wrote a strange, tired play – technically more wooden than any of his earlier work, yet pervaded with a sense of the theatre just the same – called *Il Ventaglio* or 'The Fan'. The Count always has his head in a book of fables; he shouts at the apothecary for pounding at his bronze mortar, at the shoemaker who is mending his shoes for him. He must have peace and quiet; contemporary life must never encroach on him. Like many another count in Goldoni's work he is almost penniless. As the apothecary tells him, he is alive thanks to his drugs, but he never pays for them. He has shoes thanks to the shoemaker, but he never pays for them. Asked whether the book is something rhetorical the count says 'Pooh!'; then, is it a philosophical work? – 'Pooh!' again; is it poetry? – 'Pooh!' In fact the book is 'a miracle, translated from the French'. It is a picture of nobility down at heel, cold and tired in its imagination, effete.

He may have meant it as a caricature of Gozzi (whose name was *Il Solitario* at the Testicular Academy, and whom La Tron always called 'bear'), but as a picture of a prevalent Venetian state of mind it was much more to the life. Venetian thought was tittle-tattle – spiritualism

L

and pseudo-rationalism and radical French ideas sitting side by side with the most charming superstition. No real problems disturbed the splendid somnolence.

Perhaps it was this that drove Gasparo Gozzi, Carlo's brother, to try suicide after a lifetime of writing. He turned out little essays, epithalamia, sermons, quips, plays, novels, hurrying to the printers night and day. It was as if he was searching for a real subject all his life, and never found it. He was one of the most delightful aspects of the Venetian somnolence, bent, distant, lazily well-disposed to every one. His *Gazzetta Veneta*, one of the three papers he managed at different times, ran for a year (1760) with great success, winning with its clear, easy, deft style touched with whimsy. '*Addì 8, la notte, un facchino del Fontico,addormentatosi sopra una finestra,molto ben pieno di vino, cadde giú da quella, e s'intranse, allagando tutto il terreno di sangue.*' ('On the night of the 8th a porter from the Fontico, falling asleep at the window and being very full of wine, fell outside and passed away, covering the pavement with blood.') It was not all in that modern vein. The subjects were fanciful too, and literary. It all had a light, anecdotal humour, lacking in bite and vigour. Its pages read as if a problem had never existed – only the safe city with its absorbing daily life ; what happened on one side of town was so absorbing that it had to be reported to the other.

'*Addí 16 di febbraio si vide per la prima volta questa commedia rappresentata nel teatro di San Luca*' – on 16 February 1760, Goldoni's *I Rusteghi* was seen for the first time ; Gasparo found the fact that the boors of the play were four and not one a pleasant departure from the usual comic form established by Plautus and Molière, who concentrated a dramatic theme in one principal character. The play lacked 'plebeian expressions and wretched idiocies' (implying that you could see plenty of both in the other theatres). Considering that Gasparo was a member of the Testicular Academy the praise he gives the play is objective and just to the last word. To Pietro Chiari's *La Serva Senza Padrone* in the same number he gives only a few lines, noting that the performance of this five-act piece in Martellian verse was well received 'despite the fact that the genius of the author is more inclined to the imitation of the great and resounding than the quiet'.

Much of the *Gazzetta* is imagination gone to seed. As in Pietro Chiari's work, there is whimsy and fantasy: just as Chiari describes how he pulls a scholar out of an inkpot with his finger, Gaspare gives a discussion between Ulysses and a bat; all life is a bit of a fable. The endless printed arguments about Petrarch or Dante or Homer were the highest of what went on, but even they had something petty and ineffectual about them, as if no better tittle-tattle could be found.

Since action was denied by the dream-like state of the city, nearly everyone wrote. There was hardly a housewife, a gondolier, a doctor, lawyer, coffee-house layabout who did not write. The paralysis of society, closed in a pattern decided by the past but without function for the future, was so complete that anyone who felt himself to have had a special experience (and everybody naturally did) wanted to put it down on paper for other people to know about. That this had nothing to do with writing in the proper sense made no difference to the products being bought and sold like fashion cutouts. The sleepiest people can move a pen along a page: so the city clamoured with a spurious literary vitality. Energies which could no longer be turned to great action survived on this little literary stage, craving to be recognised, though there was no one left to recognise it. Everybody was a poet, just as everybody was fashionable – just as everybody cleverly saw through the fashions he did not happen to share. So nearly everything written was just an aspect of wounded pride, an expectation of greatness drawn from centuries of great power. As to what made a writer, what conscious aptitude there had to be in him from the earliest childhood, no one cared because even as a concept the writer had ceased to exist. Eighteenth-century Venice had perhaps one born writer, in all that ocean of hack-work: Goldoni. And his work was really a steady refusal to be an artist. It was unthinkable at this time that problems of the kind that had troubled Dante and Petrarch and Tasso should be approached in writing: now stage tricks (*colpi di teatro*, in which Chiari excelled) and contrived styles that caught the eye took the place of any analysis of life. That personal, direct tone of poetry, hushed, trembling with sense –

> *Ma ben veggio or sì come al popol tutto*
> *favola fui gran tempo : onde sovente*
> *di me medesmo meco mi vergogno ;*

('But I can well see what a legend I was to everyone, for so long ; for which I am often ashamed, inside myself') – could hardly come from people who were never alone, whose heads buzzed with gossip.

Perhaps only Gasparo achieved even a hint of that tone, in his *Dodici Sermoni* :

> *Mentre che nel Friuli in mezzo a' monti*
> *Pien d'opra e di pensier, tu passi i giorni*
> *Uom da faccende ; io inutile vita, in barca*
> *Consumo il tempo, o per le vie passeggio.*

'While you pass your days in Friuli in the mountains, full of duties and worries, a man of affairs, I lead a useless life, wasting time in a boat, or taking strolls.'

Problems were a foreign import. This is why Giuseppe Baretti caused such alarm when he arrived in Venice in the sixties, bringing a serious tone for the first time, a genuine criticism. His *La Frusta Letteraria* ('The Literary Scourge') put the *Gazzetta Veneta* and the *Osservatore* in the shade. This friend of Johnson, Garrick, Mrs Thrale and Sir Joshua Reynolds was never naturalised an Englishman but he wrote and talked like one, and he died in London. He was even put on trial for murdering a ponce in Conduit Street, and was acquitted after his friends testified to his 'humanity and learning' ('never did such a constellation of genius enlighten the awful Sessions House', said Boswell). His enthusiasm for England is explained partly by the political despotism in Italy at that time: but above all he found the right problems, through its freedom. He made it clear for the first time that perhaps the fear of touching on politics and religion in Venice, bred into the citizens through the centuries, was what had robbed it of a literature.

Baretti was a debunker of 'pastorals'. He was the fearless and scathing editor of a periodical which he carried from one Italian town to another, always pursued by the censors. The Venetian government was a little more lenient, but not much: and its spies once chased him all the way to London. It was England that recognised his literary gifts, Johnson and his friends who secured him a royal pension. Among the Italian princes he never found a patron, although he looked hard enough. By nature he was excitable, impetuous, an extremist – just what no Italian government of the time wanted. He was consistent about almost nothing, including his own birth. His mind was quick, clear, able. The gambling and late nights in Venice were not at all to his taste: what he did love there was the family life, and above all the literary world that centred on the cafés, and which he could singe and tail-twist at pleasure. He knew Gaspare Gozzi and became a member of the Granelleschi; he joined in the fights against the Arcadians and what he called *frugonisms*, those affectations which were the special pride of Frugoni.

He loved the battles, the spite and envy. He described the poet Schiavo as having a great, fat, ugly moon-face like a melon, a pair of huge blear-eyes apparently lined with ham, and a head covered with long, lank, blackish, whitish, yellowish hair. Schiavo's offence had been to answer one of his sonnets with a better one of his own. Baretti's sonnet had talked about angels in heaven ringing bells for joy, and Schiavo's asked how it was possible for Baretti to have heard angels ringing bells since he knew as little about divine matters as he did about literature. Baretti's ridicule made Schiavo quiver with rage in the *caffé Menegazzo*, and he never drank coffee there again. The root of the whole trouble was Schiavo's having accused Baretti of disdaining Petrarch, which was quite untrue. That was the kind of talk that made livers swell.

What brought Baretti fame was his inspired and resounding invective, especially when he had to reply to a quip. He once described himself as a fiery man whose hand could fly to his sword in a moment (a Mrs Paradise, an American lady, once tipped a pot of boiling tea over his head for a remark like that). He also said he sang 'in the French style', though Gaspare Gozzi said he had an infernal voice and called him 'that young chap from Turin'. He also translated Corneille into

Italian for a Venetian bookseller in such a short time that it could only have been bad: later a critic described Corneille as having kneeled to God and begged him not to pardon this translator.

Baretti had three great *bêtes noires* – blank verse, Goldoni and the Arcadians. He would fly into a temper whenever he heard them mentioned. The fact that he had translated the whole of Corneille into blank verse was kept out of the discussion. Another of his hates was archaeologists: in one of his numbers of *La Frusta Letteraria* he offered a bunch of radishes to the archaeologist who could decipher an inscription (invented by himself). That nearly got him imprisoned in Turin: the archaeologists were as furious as most people are when they are touched on a point of weakness, and they managed to construe his insult to the professors as by inference a personal one to the king. That was Italian freedom at the time.

The idea that he should go to England was probably first suggested to him by the first Earl of Charlemont, to whom he was teaching Italian (and of whom Dr Johnson once said, 'I never but once heard him talk of what he had seen, and that was a large serpent in one of the pyramids of Egypt'). Baretti's impression of London was the opposite of Casanova's. While Casanova had seen 'pinched mouths opening to utter strident noises or eat great hunks of bread and butter and drink huge cups of tea', he saw endless charming girls and ladies on the streets, many of 'perfect beauty', though the streets were filthy and there was much traffic congestion. And he found the noise fiendish – from coaches and coachmen, from oyster sellers, postboys ringing their bells, watchmen and sweeps. Also this 'terribly profane people' did a lot of cursing. It was the opposite of Venetian sweetness. Drink and prostitution were the only pleasures left to the poor. There was a vicious atmosphere in the streets.

He described Dr Johnson as a 'real true-born Englishman' because he hated the Scotch, the French, the Dutch, the Hanoverians and indeed all European nations. Which meant that they had a lot in common, besides being two literary men in the finest and rarest sense. The temperate climate cooled Baretti's blood: 'the cider and beer have calmed me to such a degree that I hope that in a year or two I shall never laugh, except when I am absolutely forced to.' And when he left England at the end of his first visit he wrote, 'Farewell, beautiful England ; farewell, home of virtue, farewell, sink of vice.'

England had changed him. Perhaps the most important thing he said about his literary life was, 'I cannot help thinking rather in the English way and despising the men of letters who make no mental effort when they write.' He saw the piles of worthless verse from the Venetian academies with a fresh eye. And it was after his visit to England that he brought the *Frusta* into being.

That review, instilled with a mental discipline Johnson had taught him, was a mixture of the *Spectator* and the *Rambler*, with a touch of the *Idler* thrown in. He wanted it 'to spread like fire' through the Arcadian stables: the first number opened with a murderous attack on a 'History of Arcadia'. And it offered a neat picture of Venetian literature at the time – 'coarse comedies, dull tragedies, childish criticisms, trashy tales, frivolous treatises, and prose and verse of all kinds that are entirely without life.'

The first number was published in Venice on 1 October 1763 as a fortnightly review. He looked forward to his literary friends contributing articles and verse just as they would have in England, but, true to the Italian tradition, they played safe and criticised him for this or that little point in the first number, waiting to see how he went down with the authorities. And of course he was soon in trouble. He had another go at the archaeologists with their absurd speculations on the Etruscan language and urns and Umbrian pottery, and the minister of state in Naples (himself an archaeologist) appealed to the Neapolitan Resident in Venice to get the review stopped. But the affair blew over, after a clever letter to the Venetian authorities from Baretti. He then turned on Goldoni and Chiari. It was the first time such criticisms had been heard in Italy : exact, concrete, exhaustive, belonging to a consciously chosen tradition, written in a lively and unacademic style.

Baretti managed to get a job at Padua university at six hundred ducats a year. He was paid for writing panegyrics for marriages and elections like everyone else (for the election of a Procurator or a Grand Chancellor you got a hundred sequins). But he was not the type to turn out harmless panegyrics for long. He had a growing army of enemies, who were only waiting for him to make a mistake. A literary squabble with a monk finally caused his review to be stopped, and he came to the conclusion that 'an enemy in Italy can do you endless harm, while your friends are of little help'. He wanted to return to England 'where the opposite is the case'. Like many Italians before and after him he found it absurd that their country should even be called Christian. In other words, he loved Italy – but had to get out just the same. The implacable state machinery had begun to work against him, and he left Venice only just in time. Venice, after all, liked men of ideas beyond its borders.

He got back to England in 1766 and paid his first debts there by writing perhaps the finest defence of Italy against mistaken criticism ever produced. His *Manners and Customs in Italy* was an immediate success. Dr Johnson said, 'His account of Italy is a very entertaining book ; and, Sir, I know no man who carries his head higher in conversation than Baretti. There are strong powers in his mind. He has not, indeed, many hooks ; but with what hooks he has, he grapples very forcibly.' Venice preferred her sleepy games to the 'young chap from Turin'.

....

The government of the Republic
OPPOSITE Doge and senators in solemn procession
OVERLEAF The Bucentoro decorated for Ascension Day

Chapter 12

....

The Last Years of the Republic

Not everyone was asleep. In the last ten or fifteen years of the century there were as many secret societies (financed by the French) as there had been Spanish agents two centuries before. Even the freemasons were used to spread the new revolutionary ideas. A lodge in the Riomarin district was discovered in 1785 ; the black curtains, the black costumes and supposed 'books of magic' belonging to it were burned in St Mark's Square, and the people, believing it to be another case of witchcraft, danced round the fire. But the freemasons involved were treated very warily : in fact no charges were brought against them. And there was nothing they could be held guilty of, except holding meetings in lugubrious surroundings.

The *caffé Ancilotto* was a favourite revolutionary meeting place ; the owners were warned by the well-known police agent of the time, Cristofolo de' Cristofoli (his name inspired a sort of genial, even cosy terror), not to open a reading room at the back as they intended to, unless they wanted to go before the Inquisitors. He also arrested a number of *Barnabotti* at another café for holding suspicious opinions.

That this was not all a game, that revolution was something to fear, even in Venice, is certain. But it was the fear of it that made her capitulate to Napoleon so easily, more than an actual danger. Revolution was never popular in Venice. Had the defence of the city against the French been left to the ordinary people they would have fought for it with their hands : they would even have fought for the nobles whom they had come rather to despise after a century of kissing and gambling.

As to whether the disgruntled *Barnabotti* would have been capable of running a revolution even under French guidance is anybody's guess. They were so used to having a grievance by this time that they never really expected to be without one. The state machine had no use for

....

A Venetian procurator

them, except when it became necessary to purchase their votes in the Great Council; and revolutionary ideas from France were simply their modern way of grumbling about it all. Then there were no longer the old restraints on speech: a bold idea would at most get you a rather fictional visit from the tall, genial, smoothly efficient Cristofoli. In the sixties there was a great fuss over the senator Querini when he banished a milliner from Venice because her work had failed to come up to his wife's expectations; the Inquisitors protected the milliner against him, bowing to public opinion. There was also a quarrel between a guild, *La Scuola Grande della Carità*, and the Inquisitors about who had the right of burying one of their rich members, they or the government. This provoked an investigation into the activities of the Ten and the Inquisitors of a thoroughness which had never been dreamed of before. The archives of the Ten were found to be in order, but those of the Inquisitors were a mess, and for a while the existence of these two bodies was in question. There was wild excitement all over Venice, and an old god appeared to be about to fall. A five-hour discussion took place in the Great Council, to decide on the future of the two bodies. But anyone who believed that the ordinary people would have been happy to be rid of them (after so many cases through the centuries when the Inquisitors had protected one of their number against a powerful man) was proved wrong: together with the richer nobles the people went wild with joy when the vote – to keep both bodies – was announced. There were over six thousand people waiting in the Piazza for the news. Fireworks were set off outside the palaces of those noblemen who had spoken up for the Ten; and ironically, with a beautiful Venetian touch, the Inquisitors whose jobs had just been rescued protected the houses of those men who had voted against them.

The Barnabotti had two outspoken leaders, Carlo Contarini and Giorgio Pisani, who were always on the attack in the Great Council urging radical reforms of the constitution, and usually ones that would favour the Barnabotti. In 1780 Pisani was elected Procurator of St Mark, in itself a proof of the growing power of the Barnabotti class. Naturally that class grew as wealth declined. Pisani openly announced

....

his intention of overthrowing the doge, the Signory and all the rich, and of introducing a new agrarian law which would benefit the poor nobles in some way. The Inquisitors seized his papers and deported him to a castle at Verona, and his comrade Contarini was put under house-arrest at Cattaro. And there the last of Venice's home-made revolutions ended.

Pisani was thought a cunning man. Like many revolutionaries he practised opportunism to the point where it tainted his moral appeal. But then most nobles thought selfishly at this time ; the selfless ones were unheard, though they did exist.

Goethe described how during his visit of 1786 he sat in a gondola feeling for a moment 'a co-master of the Adriatic' with the Venetians ; everything round him was serious, a great work of human energy, a monument not of one master but a people, and despite the thick mists and the collapse of commerce and power, and the filth in the streets (for which he had a list of sound Hessian recommendations), Venice remained as remarkable for the visitor as she had always been. In other words, he took her decline for granted. She was already in the past. Yet when he saw a procession of nobles in the square he found them upright and mellow, their faces full of good-humoured magnanimity, little different from what they must have looked a couple of centuries before.

It almost seems that the Republic's fall did not really hurt or touch Venice – that she wished with all her heart to pass on to her next identity. She had an intense desire for liberation. That was the key to the ardent gambling, the collapse of responsibility. Everybody wanted to throw off the past – to be himself. Thus the nobles, who started this movement, created the revolutionary feeling they had most to fear from. With an empire behind it, Venetian society had become over the centuries highly exclusive. And there was general unspoken agreement to break this down.

The outside world had – to Venetians with eyes – begun to look more exciting ; and the atmosphere in Venice shrank proportionately. The theatre was still the only safe subject of conversation, but the punishment for rash beliefs was theatrical too. Though on paper you could get life-imprisonment for playing *panfil*, nobody did. Everyone was a little tired of it all. The only extremes you could really go to were in pleasure and tearing other people's characters to pieces. Perhaps the last really universal feeling of a fallen empire is the desire to keep your head – and if possible everyone else's – down.

The doge Paolo Renier, himself as much an enigma as the city, said in 1780, 'If there is a state in the world which absolutely needs harmony at home, it is us. We have no forces, on land or sea. We have no alliances. We live by luck, by chance, and entirely depend on the idea of Venetian prudence which other people have about us.' He died the year the French revolution began.

The election of his successor, the last doge of all, Ludovico Manin (the first to come from the 'new' moneyed nobles, whose forbears had bought their way into the Golden Book), caused so much alarm that even his wife hid herself in Murano and failed to take up the full splendour of her office. His portrait in the Museo Correr shows him looking hesitant and weak, as alarmed by what he has taken on his shoulders as most other people. He was generous with his money (that in any case was a necessary quality in a modern doge) and he rarely told a lie ; and, after all, what he did in closing the life of the Republic was the declared, almost unanimous will of the Great Council. The doge Renier had warned this council of what would happen to Venice at the hands both of powerful neighbours and powerful new ideas ; she must have allies. Instead of finding them she became more insular, more defensive. Government agents scoured the coffee houses for dangerous sounding utterances. Books and plays were censored ; any ardent discussion, on the most harmless subjects, was felt to be dangerous. The politicians argued that neutrality would see them through the dangers, as it had done for two centuries. They maintained this even after the French Revolution had started. They repeated it even when Napoleonic troops entered Italy ; they clung to it when French troops were within a mile or so of the city. Not one of them was really stupid enough to believe that neutrality could buy off either Austria or France : the truth was that they were frightened. The fear written across Manin's face, in his portrait, is fear of revolution. In the last years of the Republic the nobles thought only about themselves, what they stood to lose in the event of an uprising, not about their own loyal people, much less about the future of Venice. They knew what they could gain from Napoleon, what an excellent insurance policy he would be against the revolution he pretended to represent. And he helped them to play their game. He was careful not to betray his hostility to the Serenissima until he was close and powerful enough to spring on her effectively. Revolution, therefore, had no time to develop in Venice, before French troops were in the Piazza.

The Republic fell for the same reason that the *ancien régime* fell everywhere in Europe: no allowance was made in her government for the existence of the middle classes. That the Venetian middle class had no political ambitions, that it aped the nobility and thought them the best people to govern, simply meant that in Venice there was a vacuum where in other countries there was a bitter struggle for power. The merchants and bankers had become the core of Venice's remaining strength; this was no longer in the hands of naval commanders, ambassadors. Yet the new middle-class energies were not used to forge new political ideas. The Venetian middle class was a number of separate families, each one seemly, devout, respectable, but with no political training, no sense of responsibility beyond money-making and match-making. They were the missing link in the city's crisis.

When the government suddenly took fright and closed the cafés, because of the discussions going on in them, Angelo Maria Labia printed a savage little piece which went very roughly like this: 'Whoever wants to reform the country should not begin with the coffee houses; when trying to contain water or grain in a receptacle you think of the big stuff, not every little drop that gets lost'; and then

Xe andà in disuso l'abito patrizio,
Le Dame a forza de gran pizzegoni
De negro no le ga che qual servizio;
Ziogo e lusso spuar ne fa i polmoni,
La Religion xe andada in precipizio;
E i café fe' serar? o che . . . !

'Noblemen no longer wear their togas of office, the women have arses black from all the pinches they get; there is enough joking and luxury to make you vomit; religion is going down the drain; and you close the cafés?' And his last word, to be inferred from the dots, is *cogioni*, which means 'balls' but also like *granelleschi*, 'fools'.

When the Venetian ambassador's reports on the French revolution came from Paris, followed by letters from Louis XVI saying that he had signed the new constitution for the good of his country, there was great alarm in the Senate. The French king was answered politely, though no one doubted that he was really a prisoner of the revolutionaries. The senators realised that the new Paris could never be a friend to Venice, since the word aristocracy was now a kind of personal insult in France. The ambassador in Vienna later advised them to ally themselves quickly with Austria and Piedmont, who were both taking steps to resist the imminent French invasion. But they chose inaction.

Even when the French army was winning in Savoy they did nothing. Not that their neutrality was real. They allowed Austrian supplies to pass through Venetian territory, and they set up the French Pretender at Verona. When in 1795 France threatened a retaliatory war they replied that the Republic had an ancient treaty with Austria which gave Vienna rights of access to the Gambara road; and as for the French Pretender, now running as full a court as Louis XVIII, with envoys from London, Moscow and Vienna, they would ask him to leave. They therefore in a very short time threw away the sympathy of both sides.

The situation was always better than Venetian fears made it. England, Russia and Austria were staunchly anti-French, anti-revolutionary. There was a lot of ridiculous diplomatic by-play when the Venetian ambassador in Paris was withdrawn to London, though Venice had been alone among the European powers in recognising the revolutionary government there. The last English minister in Venice, Worsley, urged her again and again to come out clearly against France, but she timidly stomached any insult.

Not every patrician, even those least influenced by French ideas, could say he really wanted the Republic to survive. The arrival of Napoleon on the Po offered if anything an exciting solution to his

apathy : it took the matter out of his hands. And on his side, Napoleon
worked steadily through his agents in Venice to dispel the idea that
the French were a cruel and diabolical people. These agents bribed
the Barnabotti, got among the criminal elements, and altered their
theme to one of 'liberation', that catchword of the aggressor ; Napoleon
then cleverly turned the revolution, with its hot air about the Rights
of Man, into a machine for dismantling the cumbersome *ancien régime*
and substituting methodical government.

When he threatened to burn Verona to the ground as a reprisal for
the Signory's allowing Austrian troops to take up positions in Peschiera,
the *provveditore* Foscarini, elected for the purpose, opened the gates
of the town at once. But there was still no action from the Signory.
Neither the Great Council nor the Senate met. Since the *Savi* had controlled government for years, they went on doing so. When, as early
as 1788, the ambassador in Paris had written the Senate a letter in
which he warned them accurately of the coming French revolution,
the *Savi* had thought fit not to pass the letter on. Their only consistent
idea seemed to be to prevent news of Venice's dangers seeping down
to other classes. A few men at the top held an alarmed and secret
meeting at the casino Pesaro, but they dispersed with nothing decided.

For Napoleon himself the whole thing was little more than a joke.
The Serenissima was at best a means of making money for him – to
pay for his campaign. He said so in as many words : he would beat the
Austrians and make Venice pay for it. And this is what he did. It was
only the Venetians who took their power seriously.

Some patricians wanted to prepare for a siege, others wanted to give
in without admitting so ; and the third part wanted a good time at any
cost. All feared revolution. There was trouble everywhere in the
Venetian territories on the mainland, stirred by the French. In 1796
Napoleon occupied Crema, Brescia, Bergamo. But even this could have
been turned to Venice's advantage. The peasants in these districts were
all solidly pro-Venetian. But the Signory did nothing to encourage them.
The province of Verona asked to be allowed to put a deputation before
the Signory, but the *Savi* suppressed the offer and not even the Great
Council heard about it. Thousands of volunteers came to the city from

the provinces to fight, and were sent back with the official excuse of lack of equipment. A hundred middle-class youths volunteered to arm themselves at their own expense, and even that was turned down.

Instead, the nobles accepted Napoleon's offer to 'bring order' to the Venetian provinces for the price of a million francs a month for six months. The Republic was to be allowed a free hand to deal with its own rebels. And it did deal with them. For a moment everybody was fired by this new show of energy. But it quickly aroused Napoleon's desire to provoke Venice at all costs, so as to ruin any chance of the revival of her reputation. He sent a fierce ultimatum, on some faked charges, which left him free to champion those rebels Venice had just suppressed. What he most wanted was a breach of neutrality, to give him a clear excuse for invasion. He provoked it by sending a ship called 'Liberator of Italy' to the Lido, and the result was a battle in which the captain of that vessel was killed by a ball (1797). This gave him the pretext he wanted. About the same time the Signory got wind of the fact that he had signed a secret document with the Austrians ceding all the Venetian territories enclosed by the Po, the Oglio and the Adriatic coast to Vienna. There was panic. The Great Council was suddenly meeting every day. No stranger was to be allowed in the city. The Inquisitors were bent on defending the harbour.

Padua and Verona threw out their Venetian governors, and Napoleon's threats mounted to a premeditated climax. He asked the two Venetian envoys who came to see him in Graz for twenty-two million lire from the Mint, and all English drafts in the city. This was before the news of the Lido battle reached him. On 29 April 1797, French troops occupied the Venetian borders. General Baraguay d'Hilliers actually entered Venice without troops and stayed at the best hotel, under Napoleon's orders. That was how far the Signory's decree forbidding entrance to strangers worked.

The government was so used to its own procedures that it simply could not understand how discussion and decreeing were not the same as action. Then the booming of guns interrupted nervous meetings of the *Savi* in the doge's private apartments. A message came from Condulmer, in charge of the lagoon, to say that the French were preparing a sea-approach to the harbour (he later refused to defend it against them). It was now that the doge made one of the most in-effectual remarks in history: 'Tonight we are not safe in our beds'. The Procurator Pesaro went one better than that by saying, in tears, that 'one might as well be in Switzerland for all the future Venice has!'. He was the first to escape; he went to Istria and ended up in Vienna.

There was a majority vote in the Great Council for a new democratic form of government on the lines suggested by Napoleon. Next day, on 1 May, the doge explained matters to the Great Council in such a way that they voted 598 'yeas' to 21 'nays' that two deputies should be sent to Napoleon to discuss these constitutional changes. Angelo Giacomo Giustiniani (his surname perhaps the most heroic in Venetian history) was one of them: he offered himself to Napoleon as a hostage in place of his city, and Napoleon was so astounded by this zeal that he promised to save Giustiniani's property even if he should confiscate that of all the Venetian noblemen.

One of Napoleon's conditions was the suppression and trial of the Inquisitors. On 4 May the doge proposed the impeachment of these three officials; and this piece of dirty business was carried in the Great Council by seven hundred votes against twenty-four. The officials were taken to the island of S. Giorgio; and in the meantime all the Signory's political prisoners were released.

All classes were now exasperated by the government, or lack of it. A Venetian grocer called Tommaso Zorzi, the leader (so to speak) of the French revolution in Venice and living by French money, asked for a place in the government, and the *Savi* used their last diplomatic energies in persuading him and his French associates to 'postpone' revo-lution, while Napoleon no doubt was laughing his head off. The Slavonic mercenaries in the city 'irritated' the French minister, and to oblige him the Signory ordered them out, under a Morosini; thus, they volun-tarily banished their last means of self-defence.

They bribed the French agents, but ineffectively. Conspirators even got into the doge's private apartments. At one of the sittings of the Great Council another ultimatum from Napoleon was read in the form of a bill proposing a new provisional government. Just after the reading

M

there was a discharge of musketry close to the doors of the palace, as it seemed. In panic the members divided, and this time it was 513 'yeas' to 30 'nays' and 5 blanks. Then, having signed themselves out of office, they all ran away home.

The musketry had been the parting salute of the Slavonic troops, a mark of respect for the Serenissima. It left government in the hands of the people. They burned down Zorzi's house with cries of '*Viva San Marco!*' and on the nights of 12 and 13 May there was terrible confusion everywhere in the city. The 'riot' was put down, since there was still a police force. On the 15th the French came in. The next day two notices were put up in the Piazza, one saying that the Great Council yielded its powers to a provisional government, the other praising the Great Council for resigning and also for putting down the 'riot'. And there was some stuff about liberty, equality and fraternity.

The people knew perfectly well who had handed them over to the French. They stood outside the noble houses screaming '*Assassini di San Marco!*' ('Murderers of St Mark!'). Bernardino Renier's answer was to sweep the streets with artillery. Like his cousin, Giustinia, who had filled the office of dogaressa under her uncle Paolo, he hoped that Napoleon would rescue Venice from her ruin. What Napoleon did was to hand her over to the Austrians, lock, stock and barrel.

The words '*Pax tibi Marce*' were scratched off the stone lions of the city and 'Rights and Duties of Man and Citizen' substituted. The lion on the left column of the Piazzetta was pulled down. On 4 June a tree of liberty was raised in the middle of the Piazza, and a nearby fire burned the Golden Book and the ducal insignia, between two statues representing Freedom and Equality. The three Inquisitors were tried and found guilty, and then pardoned by Napoleon. On 17 October the treaty of Campo Formio sold Venice and all its territory to Austria. The Byzantine horses of St Mark were removed to Paris. And in the middle of the first month of 1798 the Austrian garrison took over.

It had been called the age of reason, except that the nobles had understood nothing of what was going on. Like Catherine the Great they talked liberal reform while the real state of their country was hidden from them, and then, like her, like Casanova, like Ippolito

Pindemonte who had written an ode on the French Revolution, they were scandalised by what happened in Paris. But whereas in France there was an energetic, politically minded middle class to take over government, in Venice the nobles were all the government there was. They were the Republic. And so the Republic fell.

BIBLIOGRAPHY

....

M. S. Anderson, *Europe in the Eighteenth Century* (Longmans, London, 1961).

Auguste Bailly, *Le Sérénissime République de Venise* (1946).

Auguste Bazzoni, *Le Annotazione degli Inquisitori di Stato* (Archivio Storico Italiano, Florence, 1870).

William Beckford, *Italy* (1834).

Daniele Beltrami, *Storia della Popolazione di Venezia* (Collana Ca' Foscari, Padua, 1954).

Marino Berengo, *La Società Veneta alla fine del Setteconto* (Florence, 1956).

Berenson, *Italian Painting of the Renascence* (Clarendon Press, Oxford, 1930).

Giuseppe Bernoni, *Canti Popolari Veneziani* (Venice, 1872); *Preghiere popolare* (Venice, 1873); *Fiabe e Novelle Popolare Veneziani* (Venice, 1873).

Edmond Bonnal, *Chute d'une République* (Paris, 1885).

Marcel Brion, *Venice* (Elek Books, London, 1962).

Charles de Brosses, *L'Italie* (Paris, 1836).

H. R. F. Brown, *Venetian Studies* (Kegan Paul and Co., London, 1887); *Life on the Lagoons* (Kegan Paul and Co., London, 1884); *In and Around Venice* (Rivingtons, London, 1905); *Studies in the History of Venice* (John Murray, London, 1907); *Venice* (Percival and Co., London, 1893); *Calendar of State Papers relating to English Affairs in the Archives of Venice* (1864); *The Venetian Republic* (J. M. Dent and Co., London, 1902).

Charles Burney, *Musical Tour* (T. Becket and Co., London, 1771); *History of Music* (London, 1776).

Casanova Confidente degli Inquisitori di Stato (Nuovo Archivio Veneto, Florence, 1894).

Gian Giacomo Casanova, *Histoire de ma Vie* (ed. Brockhaus, Paris, 1960–2).

Rosalba Carriera, *Diario* (Venice, 1865).

Conte de Caylus, *Voyage d'Italie, 1714–15* (Paris, 1914).

Giovanni Comisso, *Agenti Segreti Veneziani nel 700* (1945).

James R. Childs, *Casanova* (Allen and Unwin, London, 1961).

F. Marion Crawford, *Gleanings from Venetian History* (Macmillan and Co., London, 1905).

Pietro Chiari, *Commedie da Camera* (Venice, 1771).

Conte Daru, *Histoire de la république de Venise* (Paris, 1821).

E. J. Dent, *Alessandro Scarlatti* (Edward Arnold, London, 1905).

John Evelyn, *Memoirs* (H. Colburn, London, 1818).

Urbani de Gheltof, *Le Maschere in Venezia* (1877).

Wolfgang Goethe, *Italienische Reise* (Leipzig, 1925).

Carlo Goldoni, *Le Théâtre et la Vie en Italie au XVIIIe* (Paris, 1896); *Comédie* (1823).

R. S. Gower, *Selections from the letters of de Brosses* (Kegan Paul and Co., London, 1897).

Carlo Gozzi, *Memorie Inutile* (1797); *Fiabe* (Bologna, 1884).

Gasparo Gozzi, *Opere* (Padua, 1818); *Dodici Sermoni* (Bologna, 1763); *La Gazzetta Veneta* (Sansoni, Florence, 1957).

Pier Antonio Gratarol, *Narrazione Apologetica* (Venice, 1797); *Memorie Ultime* (1797).

W. Carew Hazlitt, *The History of the Venetian Republic* (A. and C. Black, London, 1900).

Edward Hutton, *Venice and Venetia* (Methuen and Co., London, 1954).

Norbert Jonard, *La Vie Quotidienne à Venise du XVIIIe Siècle*.

Angelo Maria Labia, *Opere* (1817).

Vernon Lee, *Studies of the Eighteenth Century in Italy* (W. Satchell and Co., London, 1880).

Antonio Longhi, *Memoria della Vita* (1820).

A. Machen, *Memoirs of Casanova* (8 vols, 1949); *Casanova's Escape* (1925).

Vittorio Malamani, *Il Settecento a Venezia* (Turin, 1891–2).

H. Mamet, *Le Président de Brosses* (Paris, 1874).

Benedetto Marcello, *Teatro alla Moda* (1733).

Giovanni Mariacher, *Ca' Rezzonico* (Ca' Rezzonico publication, 1967).

G. Mazzotti, *Le Ville Venete* (Treviso, 1953).

Pietro Metastasio, *Melodrammi* (Turin, 1796).

Pompeo Molmenti, *Venezia nella Vita Privata* (Bergamo, 1905–8); *La Dogaressa* (Turin, 1884); *Epistolari Veneziani del Secolo XVIII* (1914).

Philippe Monnier, *Venise du XVIIIe Siècle* (Paris, 1907).

Lady Mary Wortley Montagu, *Letters and Works* (R. Bentley, London, 1837).

John Moore, *A View of Society and Manners in Italy* (London, 1795).

Giuseppe Morazzoni, *La Moda a Venezia nel Secolo XVIII* (Milan, 1931).

Lacy C. Morley, *Giuseppe Baretti* (John Murray, London, 1909).

Christian M. Nebehay, *Bibliography of Casanova* (Vienna, 1956).

Ippolito Niero, *Le Memorie di un Ottogenario*.

Giuseppe Ortolani, *Voci e Visioni del Settecento Veneziano* (1926).

Mrs Margaret Oliphant, *Makers of Venice* (Macmillan and Co., London, 1887).

Lorenzo da Ponte, *Memorie* (New York, 1829).

Baron de Poelnitz, *Lettres et Mémoires* (Amsterdam, 1737).

Marc Pincherle, *Vivaldi* (Paris, 1948).

Giustina Renier-Michiel, *Origines des Fêtes Vénitiennes*.

Romain Rolland, *La Musique en Italie au XVIIIᵉ* (Revue de Paris, 1905).

Samuele Romanin, *Storia Documentata della Repubblica di Venezia* (Venice, 1853–61).

John Ruskin, *The Stones of Venice* (London, 1851–3).

John Addington Symonds, *Memoirs of Count Carlo Gozzi* (1890).

Edward Smedley, *Sketches from Venetian History* (1831).

Giovanni Tabacco, *Andrea Tron e la Crisi dell'Aristocrazia Senatoria di Venezia* (Trieste, 1957).

G. Tassini, *Sentense Capitali della Repubblica di Venezia; Curiosita Veneziane* (1913).

Mrs Hester Lynch Thrale, *Glimpses of Italian Society* (Beeley and Co., London, 1892).

Gianfranco Torcellan, *Andrea Memmo* (1957).

Touring Club Italiano, *Venezia e Dintorni* (1951).

Voltaire, *Le Siècle de Louis XIV* (1756); *Candide* (1759).

Alathea Weil, *Venice* (1894).

Simon Towneley Worsthorne, *Venetian Opera in the Seventeenth Century* (Oxford, 1954).

INDEX

....